TABLE OF CONTENTS

I0049071

#	SUBJECT	PAGE
1	YEARLY PAYMENTS & DEPOSITS SUMMARY AND CHART	1 - 2
2	MONTHLY PAYMENTS & DEPOSITS SUMMARY AND CHART	3 - 26
3	DAILY PAYMENTS & DEPOSITS	27 - 116

TABLE OF CONTENTS

#	SUBJECT	PAGE

TABLE OF CONTENTS

#	SUBJECT	PAGE

YEARLY PAYMENTS & DEPOSITS SUMMARY

YEAR : ....

MONTH	PAYMENT / DEBIT (-)	DEPOSIT / CREDIT (+)	TOTAL	NOTES
TOTAL				

NOTES

_____

_____

_____

_____

_____

_____

_____

_____

_____

_____

_____

_____

_____

_____

_____

YEARLY PAYMENTS & DEPOSITS CHART

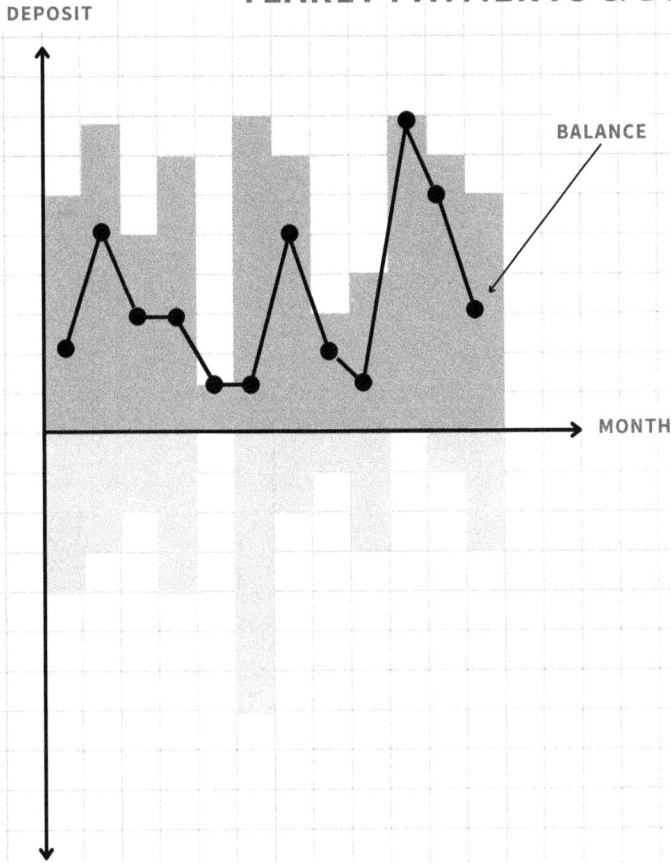

DEPOSIT

BALANCE

MONTH

PAYMENT

HOW TO:
BUILD YOUR CHART USING YOUR MONTHLY
PAYMENTS & DEPOSITS SUMMARIES:
- CALCULATE YOUR SCALE USING THE
  HIGHEST NUMBER IN TERMS OF PAYMENT OR
  DEPOSIT PER MONTH AND DIVIDE IT BY 10
  TO GET THE SIZE OF A SQUARE ON THE Y
  AXIS
- PLOT YOUR TOTAL MONTHLY DEPOSITS AS
  POSITIVE BARS ON THE Y-AXIS AND YOUR
  TOTAL MONTHLY PAYMENTS AS NEGATIVE
  BARS ON THE Y-AXIS (DIVIDE MONTHLY
  PAYMENT/DEPOSIT BY THE SIZE OF A
  SQUARE TO FIND THE NUMBER OF SQUARES
  TO FILL)
- BUILD YOUR BALANCE LINE CHART USING
  YOUR MONTHLY TOTAL

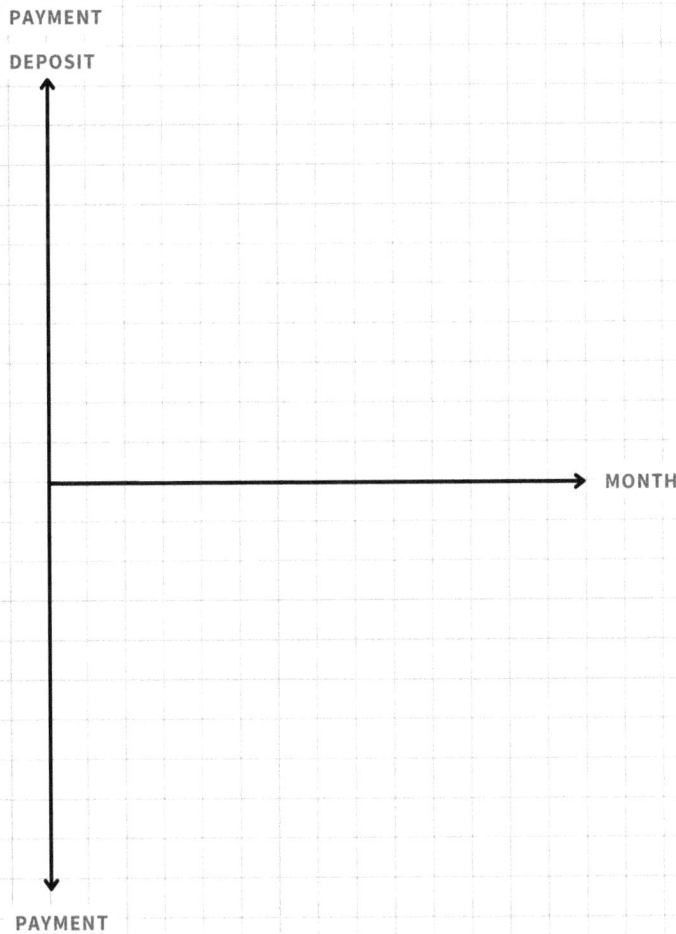

YEAR:

DEPOSIT

MONTH

NOTES:

PAYMENT

MONTHLY PAYMENTS & DEPOSITS SUMMARY

MONTH : ....

DATE	DAY	PAYMENT / DEBIT (-)	DEPOSIT / CREDIT (+)	TOTAL	NOTES
1					
2					
3					
4					
5					
6					
7					
8					
9					
10					
11					
12					
13					
14					
15					
16					
17					
18					
19					
20					
21					
22					
23					
24					
25					
26					
27					
28					
29					
30					
31					
TOTAL					

MONTHLY PAYMENTS & DEPOSITS CHART

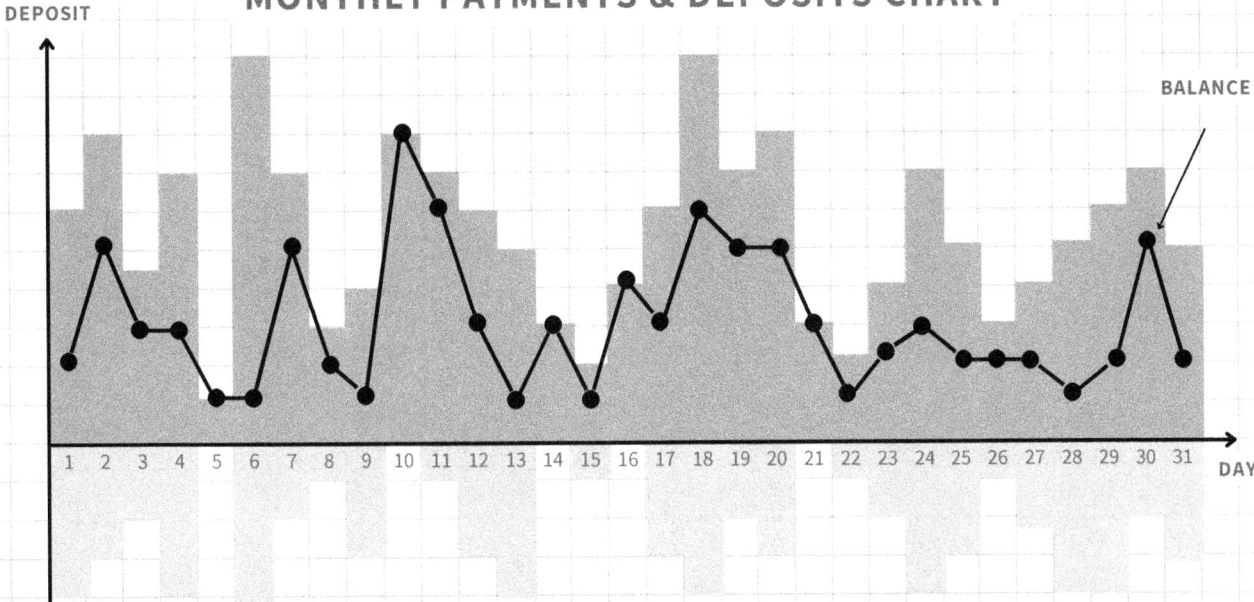

HOW TO:

BUILD YOUR CHART USING YOUR MONTHLY PAYMENTS & DEPOSITS SUMMARY:
- CALCULATE YOUR SCALE USING THE HIGHEST NUMBER IN TERMS OF PAYMENT OR DEPOSIT PER DAY AND DIVIDE IT BY 10 TO GET THE SIZE OF A SQUARE ON THE Y AXIS
- PLOT YOUR TOTAL DAILY DEPOSITS AS POSITIVE BARS ON THE Y-AXIS AND YOUR TOTAL DAILY PAYMENTS AS NEGATIVE BARS ON THE Y-AXIS (DIVIDE DAILY PAYMENT/DEPOSIT BY THE SIZE OF A SQUARE TO FIND THE NUMBER OF SQUARES TO FILL)
- BUILD YOUR BALANCE LINE CHART USING YOUR DAILY TOTAL

MONTH:

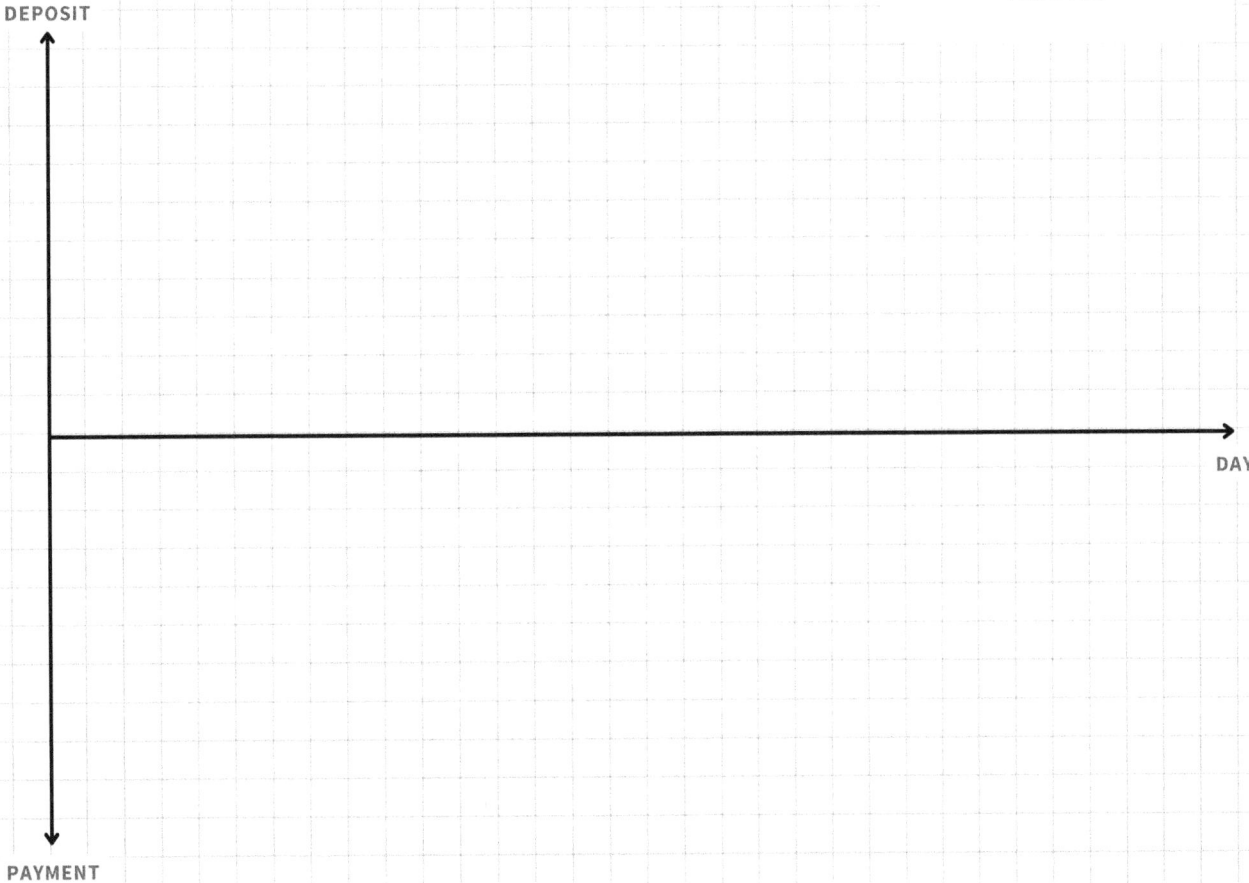

4

MONTHLY PAYMENTS & DEPOSITS SUMMARY

MONTH : ....

DATE	DAY	PAYMENT / DEBIT (-)	DEPOSIT / CREDIT (+)	TOTAL	NOTES
1					
2					
3					
4					
5					
6					
7					
8					
9					
10					
11					
12					
13					
14					
15					
16					
17					
18					
19					
20					
21					
22					
23					
24					
25					
26					
27					
28					
29					
30					
31					
TOTAL					

MONTHLY PAYMENTS & DEPOSITS CHART

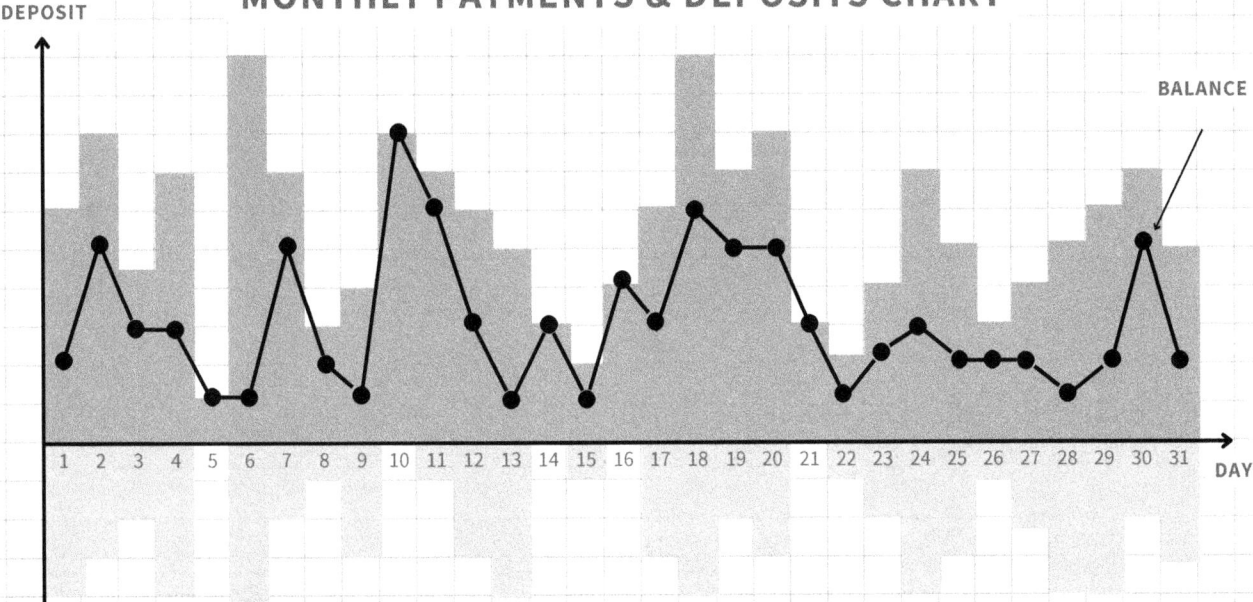

DEPOSIT

BALANCE

1 2 3 4 5 6 7 8 9 10 11 12 13 14 15 16 17 18 19 20 21 22 23 24 25 26 27 28 29 30 31 DAY

PAYMENT

HOW TO:

BUILD YOUR CHART USING YOUR MONTHLY PAYMENTS & DEPOSITS SUMMARY:

- CALCULATE YOUR SCALE USING THE HIGHEST NUMBER IN TERMS OF PAYMENT OR DEPOSIT PER DAY AND DIVIDE IT BY 10 TO GET THE SIZE OF A SQUARE ON THE Y AXIS
- PLOT YOUR TOTAL DAILY DEPOSITS AS POSITIVE BARS ON THE Y-AXIS AND YOUR TOTAL DAILY PAYMENTS AS NEGATIVE BARS ON THE Y-AXIS (DIVIDE DAILY PAYMENT/DEPOSIT BY THE SIZE OF A SQUARE TO FIND THE NUMBER OF SQUARES TO FILL)
- BUILD YOUR BALANCE LINE CHART USING YOUR DAILY TOTAL

MONTH:

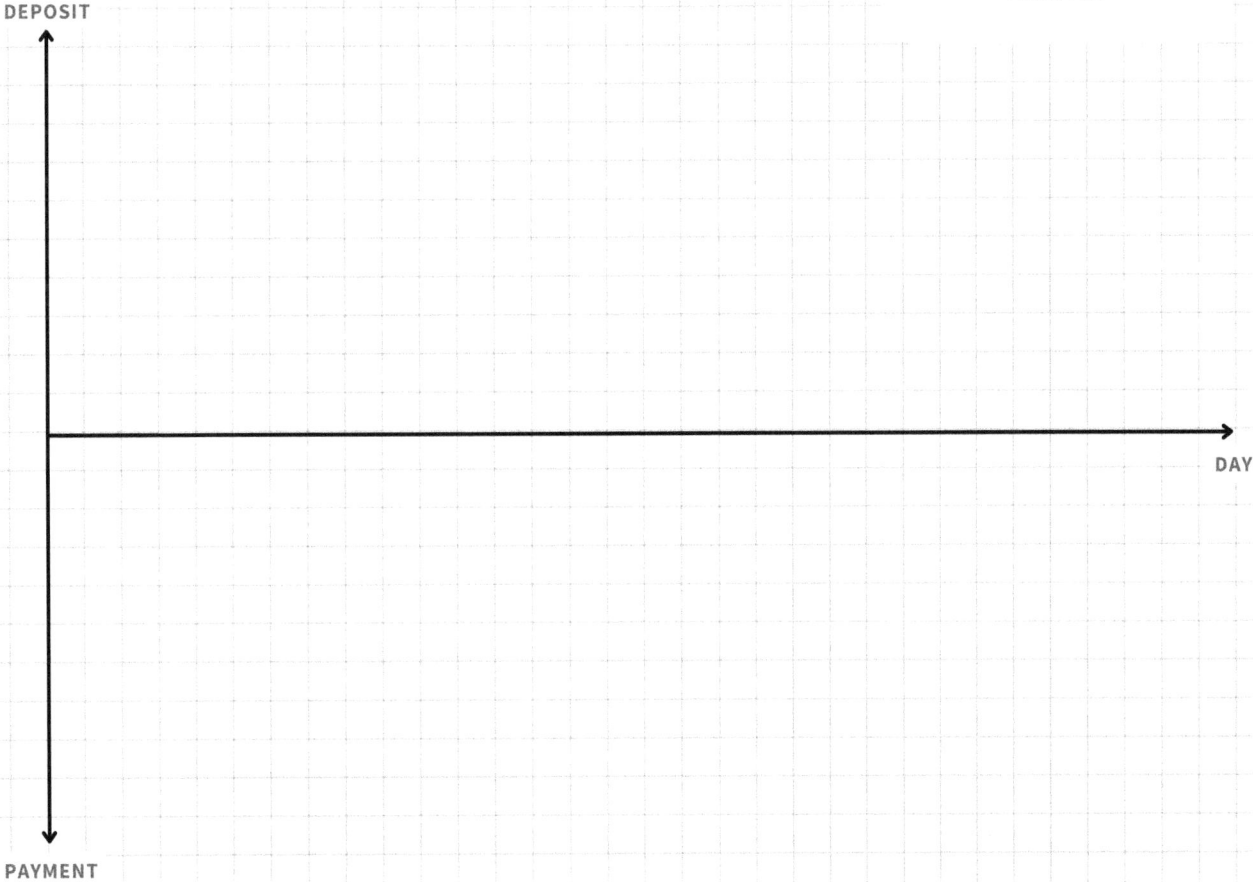

DEPOSIT

DAY

PAYMENT

MONTHLY PAYMENTS & DEPOSITS SUMMARY

MONTH : ....

DATE	DAY	PAYMENT / DEBIT (-)	DEPOSIT / CREDIT (+)	TOTAL	NOTES
1					
2					
3					
4					
5					
6					
7					
8					
9					
10					
11					
12					
13					
14					
15					
16					
17					
18					
19					
20					
21					
22					
23					
24					
25					
26					
27					
28					
29					
30					
31					
TOTAL					

MONTHLY PAYMENTS & DEPOSITS CHART

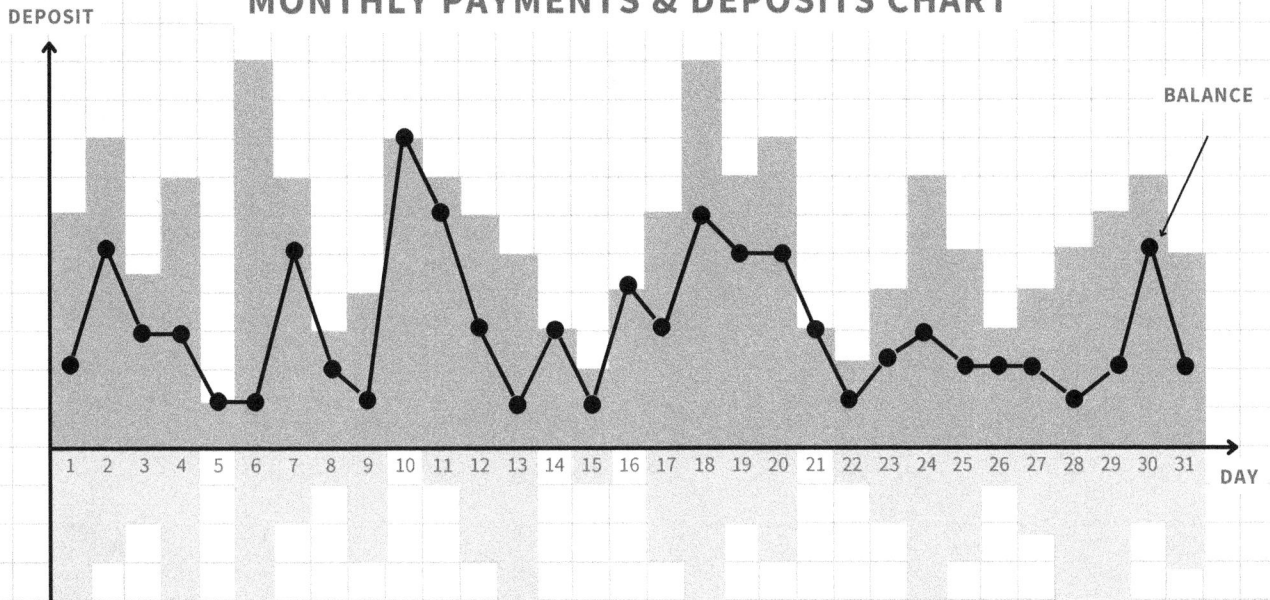

HOW TO:
BUILD YOUR CHART USING YOUR MONTHLY PAYMENTS & DEPOSITS SUMMARY:
- CALCULATE YOUR SCALE USING THE HIGHEST NUMBER IN TERMS OF PAYMENT OR DEPOSIT PER DAY AND DIVIDE IT BY 10 TO GET THE SIZE OF A SQUARE ON THE Y AXIS
- PLOT YOUR TOTAL DAILY DEPOSITS AS POSITIVE BARS ON THE Y-AXIS AND YOUR TOTAL DAILY PAYMENTS AS NEGATIVE BARS ON THE Y-AXIS (DIVIDE DAILY PAYMENT/DEPOSIT BY THE SIZE OF A SQUARE TO FIND THE NUMBER OF SQUARES TO FILL)
- BUILD YOUR BALANCE LINE CHART USING YOUR DAILY TOTAL

MONTH:

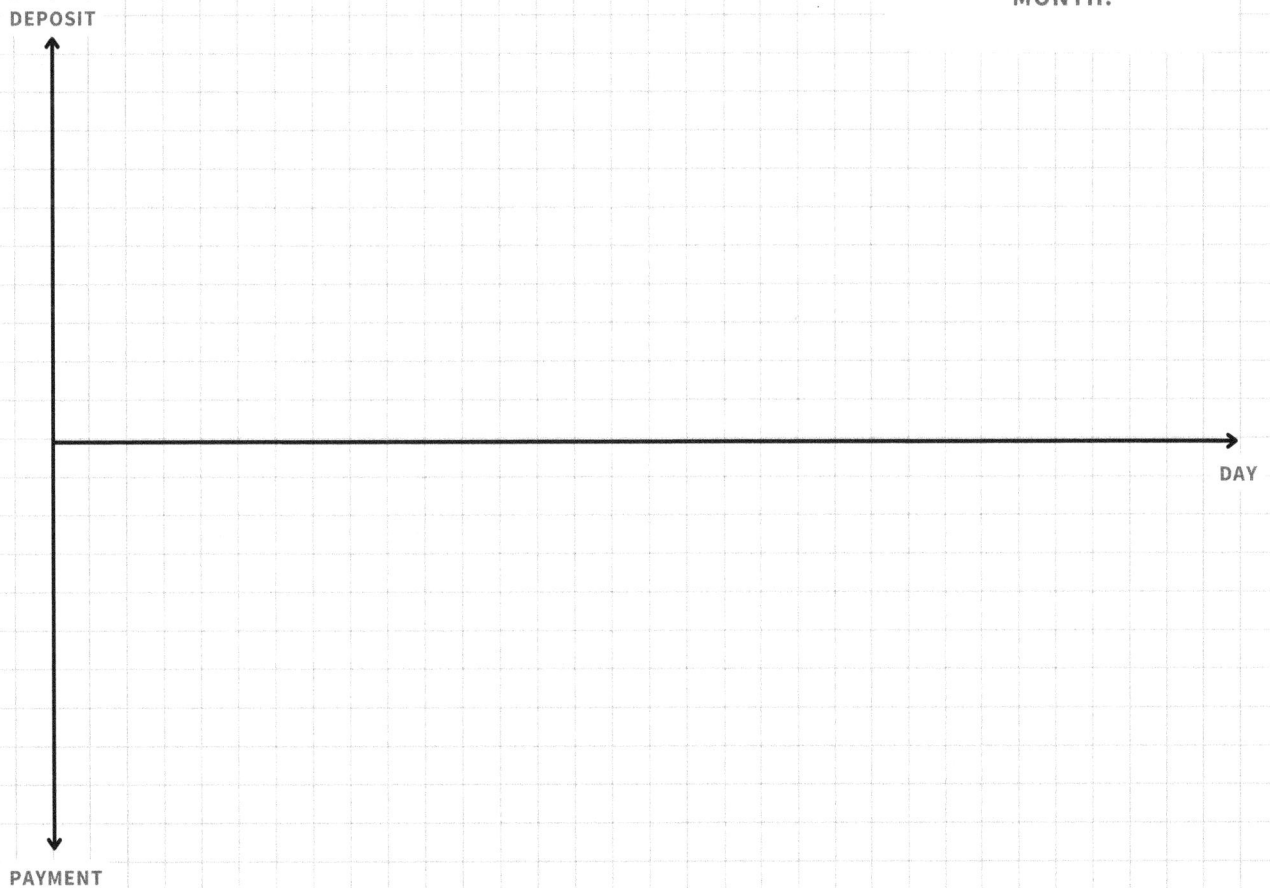

MONTHLY PAYMENTS & DEPOSITS SUMMARY

MONTH : ....

DATE	DAY	PAYMENT / DEBIT (-)	DEPOSIT / CREDIT (+)	TOTAL	NOTES
1					
2					
3					
4					
5					
6					
7					
8					
9					
10					
11					
12					
13					
14					
15					
16					
17					
18					
19					
20					
21					
22					
23					
24					
25					
26					
27					
28					
29					
30					
31					
TOTAL					

MONTHLY PAYMENTS & DEPOSITS CHART

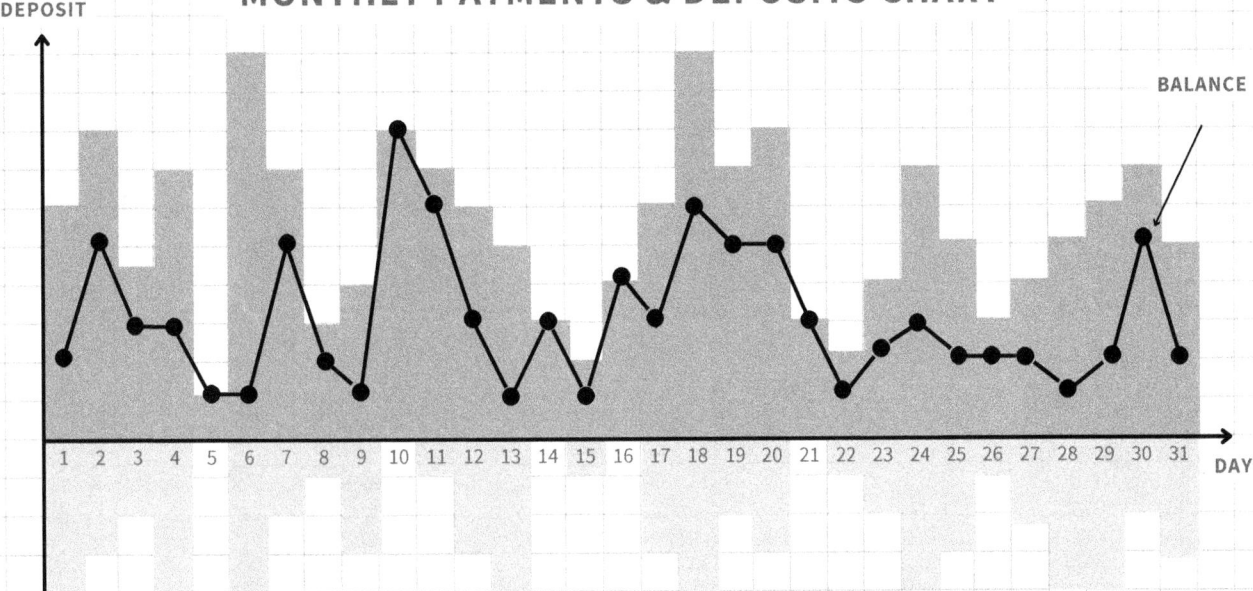

DEPOSIT

BALANCE

PAYMENT

1 2 3 4 5 6 7 8 9 10 11 12 13 14 15 16 17 18 19 20 21 22 23 24 25 26 27 28 29 30 31   DAY

HOW TO:

BUILD YOUR CHART USING YOUR MONTHLY PAYMENTS & DEPOSITS SUMMARY:
- CALCULATE YOUR SCALE USING THE HIGHEST NUMBER IN TERMS OF PAYMENT OR DEPOSIT PER DAY AND DIVIDE IT BY 10 TO GET THE SIZE OF A SQUARE ON THE Y AXIS
- PLOT YOUR TOTAL DAILY DEPOSITS AS POSITIVE BARS ON THE Y-AXIS AND YOUR TOTAL DAILY PAYMENTS AS NEGATIVE BARS ON THE Y-AXIS (DIVIDE DAILY PAYMENT/DEPOSIT BY THE SIZE OF A SQUARE TO FIND THE NUMBER OF SQUARES TO FILL)
- BUILD YOUR BALANCE LINE CHART USING YOUR DAILY TOTAL

MONTH:

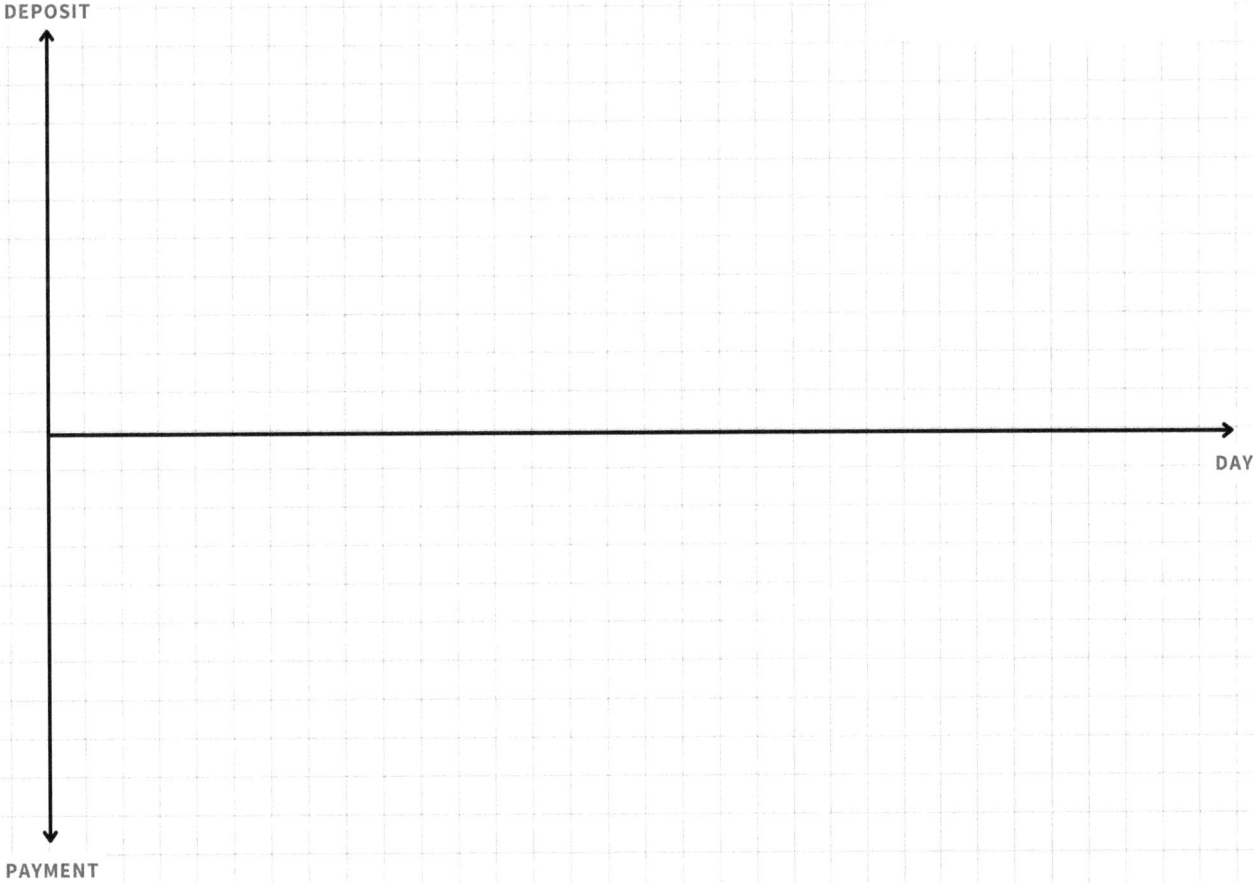

DEPOSIT

DAY

PAYMENT

10

MONTHLY PAYMENTS & DEPOSITS SUMMARY

MONTH : ....

DATE	DAY	PAYMENT / DEBIT (-)	DEPOSIT / CREDIT (+)	TOTAL	NOTES
1					
2					
3					
4					
5					
6					
7					
8					
9					
10					
11					
12					
13					
14					
15					
16					
17					
18					
19					
20					
21					
22					
23					
24					
25					
26					
27					
28					
29					
30					
31					
TOTAL					

MONTHLY PAYMENTS & DEPOSITS CHART

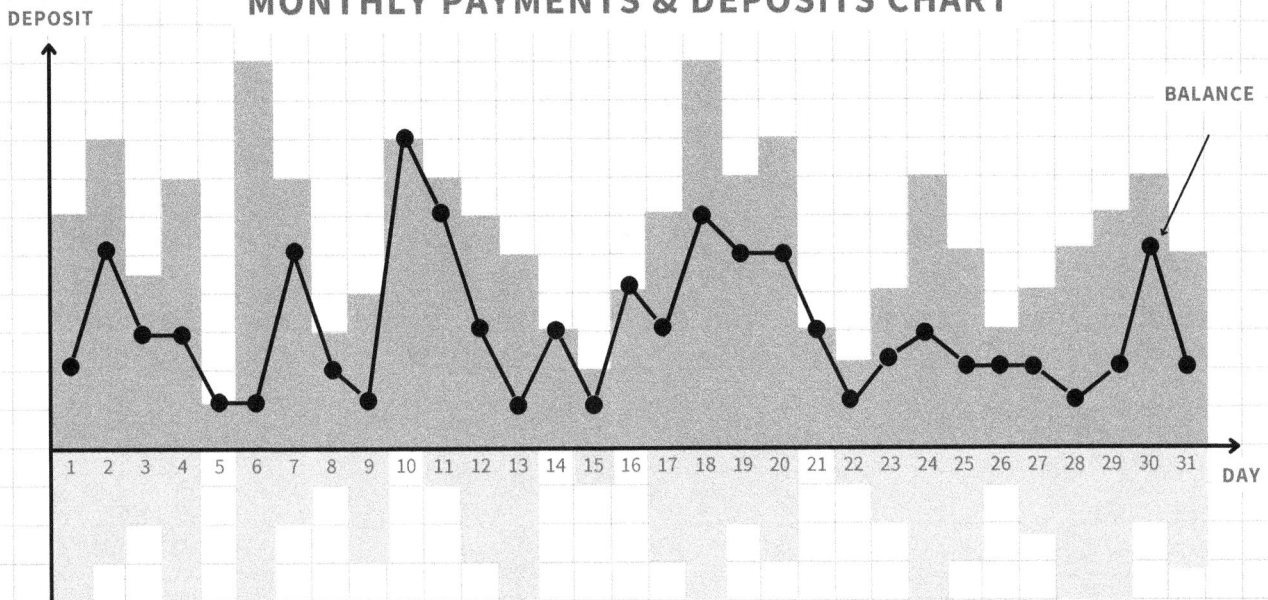

DEPOSIT

BALANCE

PAYMENT

1 2 3 4 5 6 7 8 9 10 11 12 13 14 15 16 17 18 19 20 21 22 23 24 25 26 27 28 29 30 31   DAY

HOW TO:

BUILD YOUR CHART USING YOUR MONTHLY PAYMENTS & DEPOSITS SUMMARY:
- CALCULATE YOUR SCALE USING THE HIGHEST NUMBER IN TERMS OF PAYMENT OR DEPOSIT PER DAY AND DIVIDE IT BY 10 TO GET THE SIZE OF A SQUARE ON THE Y AXIS
- PLOT YOUR TOTAL DAILY DEPOSITS AS POSITIVE BARS ON THE Y-AXIS AND YOUR TOTAL DAILY PAYMENTS AS NEGATIVE BARS ON THE Y-AXIS (DIVIDE DAILY PAYMENT/DEPOSIT BY THE SIZE OF A SQUARE TO FIND THE NUMBER OF SQUARES TO FILL)
- BUILD YOUR BALANCE LINE CHART USING YOUR DAILY TOTAL

MONTH:

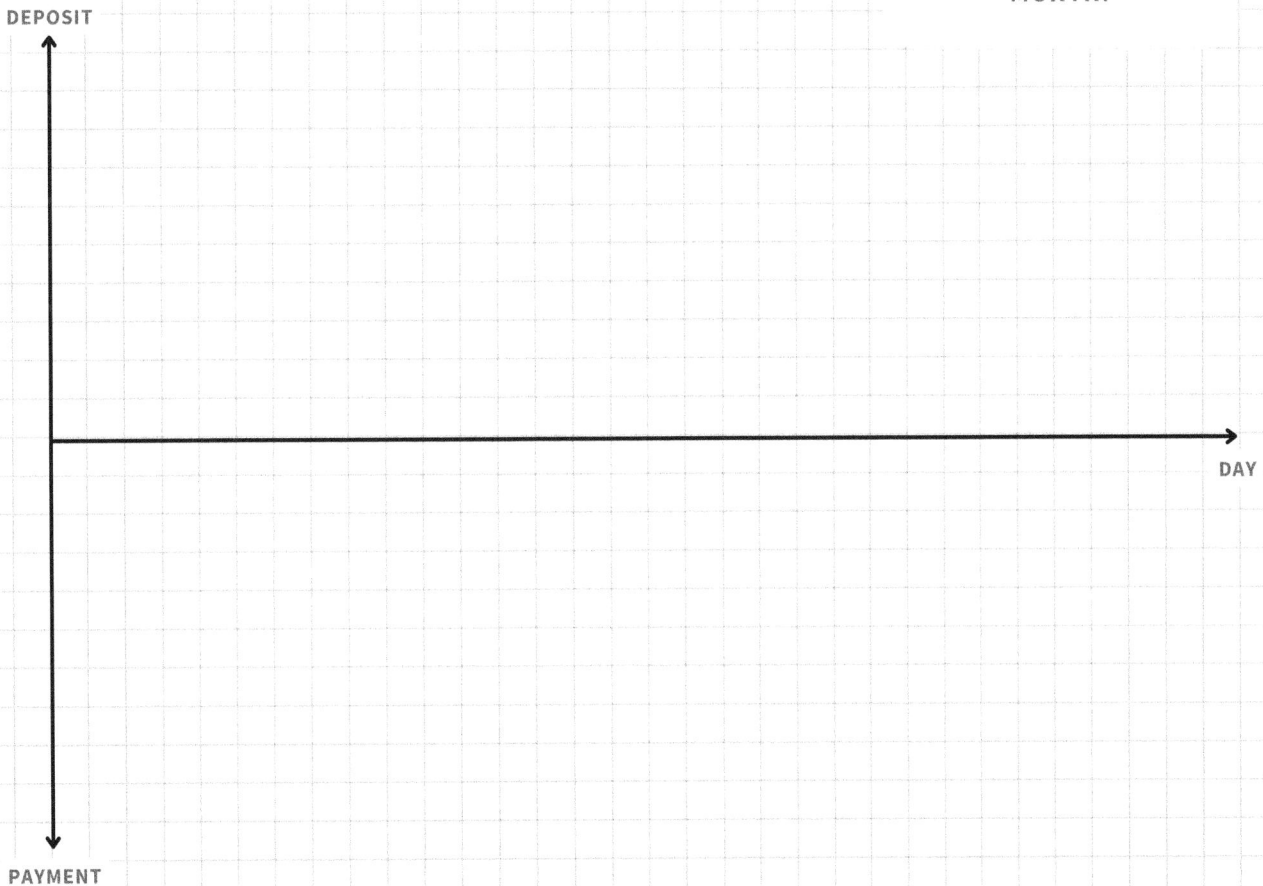

DEPOSIT

DAY

PAYMENT

MONTHLY PAYMENTS & DEPOSITS SUMMARY

MONTH : ....

DATE	DAY	PAYMENT / DEBIT (-)	DEPOSIT / CREDIT (+)	TOTAL	NOTES
1					
2					
3					
4					
5					
6					
7					
8					
9					
10					
11					
12					
13					
14					
15					
16					
17					
18					
19					
20					
21					
22					
23					
24					
25					
26					
27					
28					
29					
30					
31					
TOTAL					

MONTHLY PAYMENTS & DEPOSITS CHART

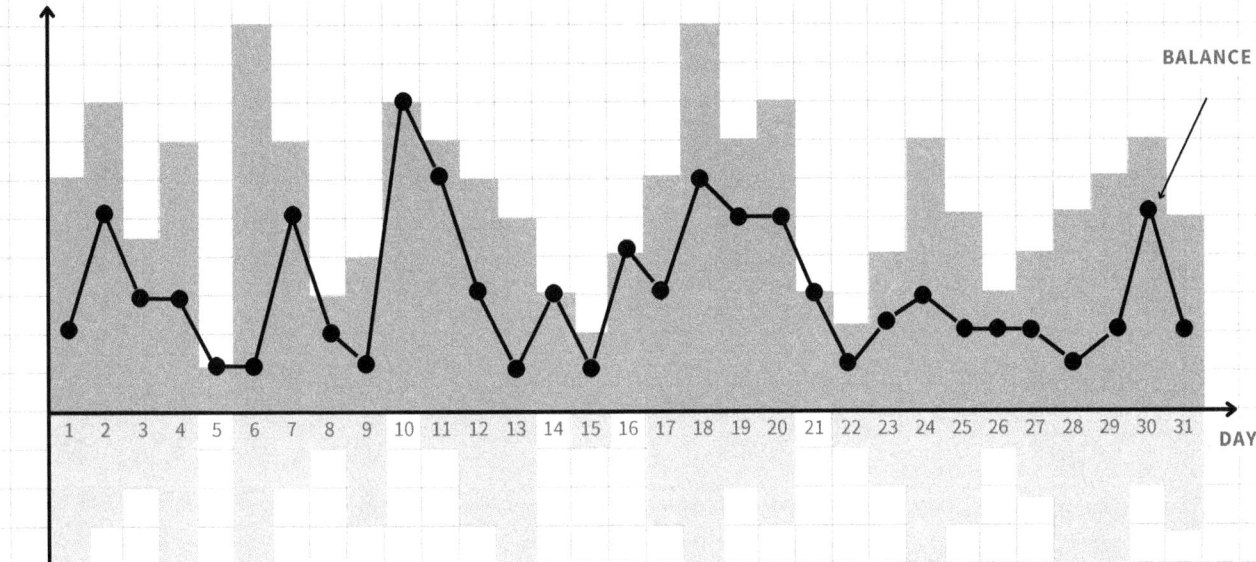

HOW TO:

BUILD YOUR CHART USING YOUR MONTHLY PAYMENTS & DEPOSITS SUMMARY:
- CALCULATE YOUR SCALE USING THE HIGHEST NUMBER IN TERMS OF PAYMENT OR DEPOSIT PER DAY AND DIVIDE IT BY 10 TO GET THE SIZE OF A SQUARE ON THE Y AXIS
- PLOT YOUR TOTAL DAILY DEPOSITS AS POSITIVE BARS ON THE Y-AXIS AND YOUR TOTAL DAILY PAYMENTS AS NEGATIVE BARS ON THE Y-AXIS (DIVIDE DAILY PAYMENT/DEPOSIT BY THE SIZE OF A SQUARE TO FIND THE NUMBER OF SQUARES TO FILL)
- BUILD YOUR BALANCE LINE CHART USING YOUR DAILY TOTAL

MONTH:

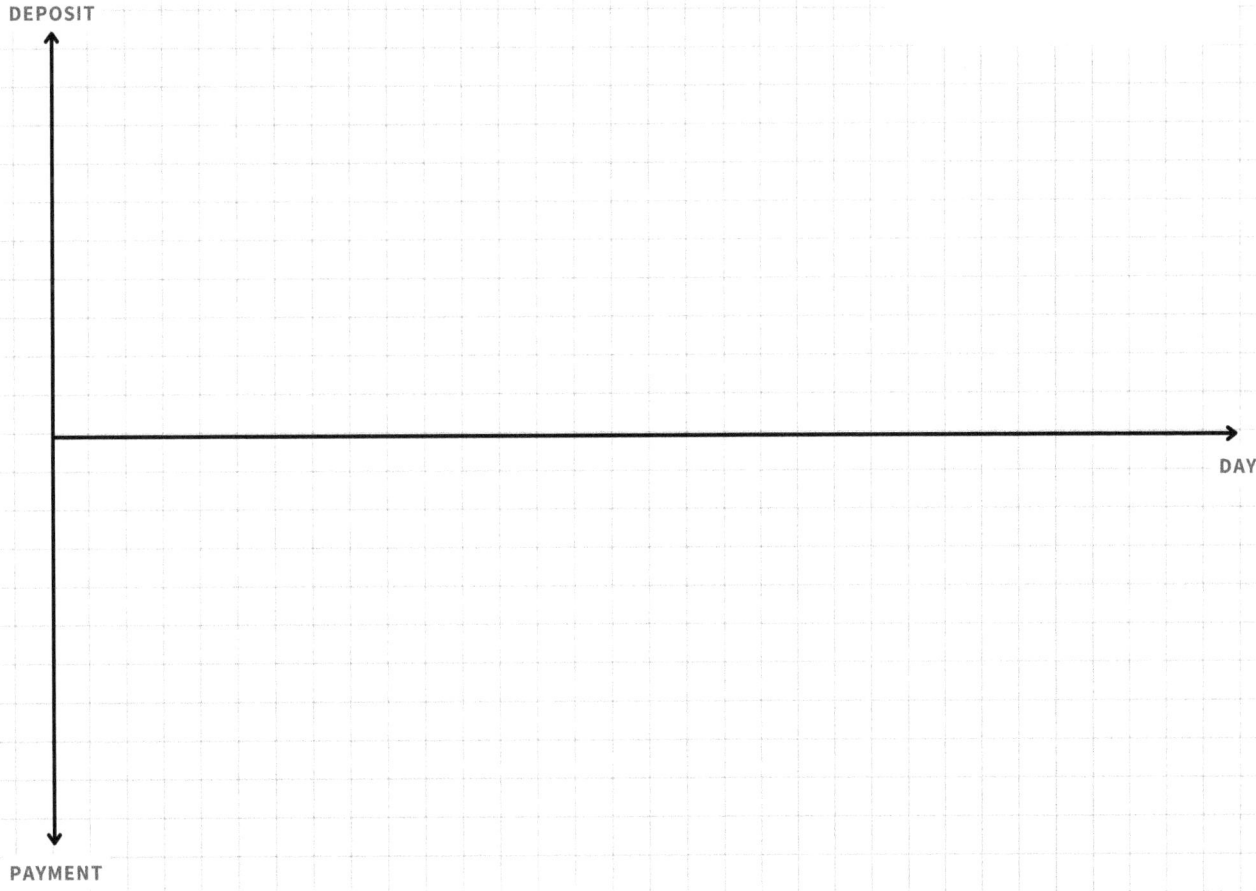

14

MONTHLY PAYMENTS & DEPOSITS SUMMARY

MONTH : ....

DATE	DAY	PAYMENT / DEBIT (-)	DEPOSIT / CREDIT (+)	TOTAL	NOTES
1					
2					
3					
4					
5					
6					
7					
8					
9					
10					
11					
12					
13					
14					
15					
16					
17					
18					
19					
20					
21					
22					
23					
24					
25					
26					
27					
28					
29					
30					
31					
TOTAL					

MONTHLY PAYMENTS & DEPOSITS CHART

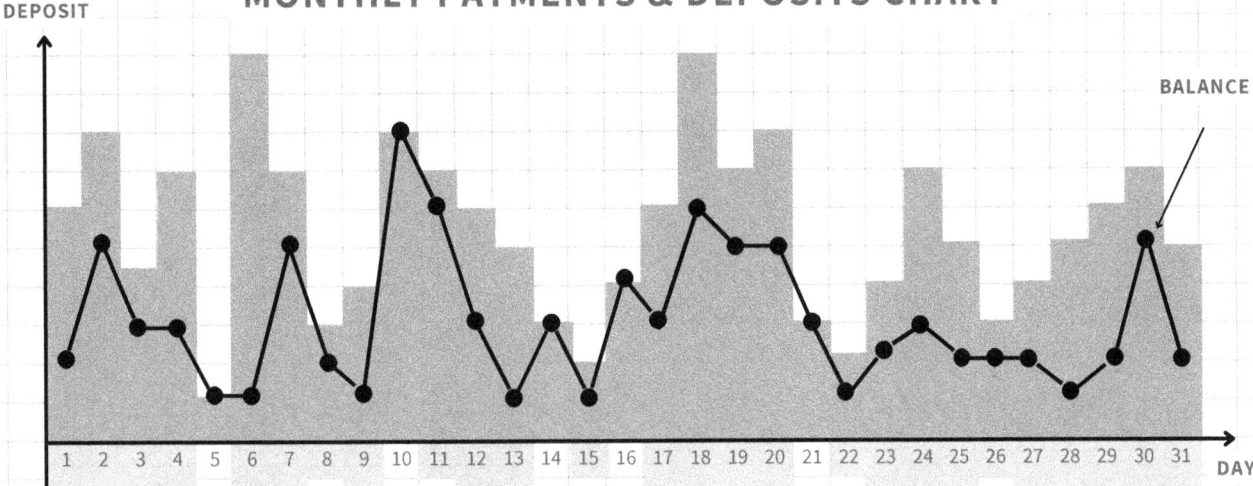

DEPOSIT

BALANCE

1 2 3 4 5 6 7 8 9 10 11 12 13 14 15 16 17 18 19 20 21 22 23 24 25 26 27 28 29 30 31 **DAY**

PAYMENT

HOW TO:
BUILD YOUR CHART USING YOUR MONTHLY PAYMENTS & DEPOSITS SUMMARY:
- CALCULATE YOUR SCALE USING THE HIGHEST NUMBER IN TERMS OF PAYMENT OR DEPOSIT PER DAY AND DIVIDE IT BY 10 TO GET THE SIZE OF A SQUARE ON THE Y AXIS
- PLOT YOUR TOTAL DAILY DEPOSITS AS POSITIVE BARS ON THE Y-AXIS AND YOUR TOTAL DAILY PAYMENTS AS NEGATIVE BARS ON THE Y-AXIS (DIVIDE DAILY PAYMENT/DEPOSIT BY THE SIZE OF A SQUARE TO FIND THE NUMBER OF SQUARES TO FILL)
- BUILD YOUR BALANCE LINE CHART USING YOUR DAILY TOTAL

MONTH:

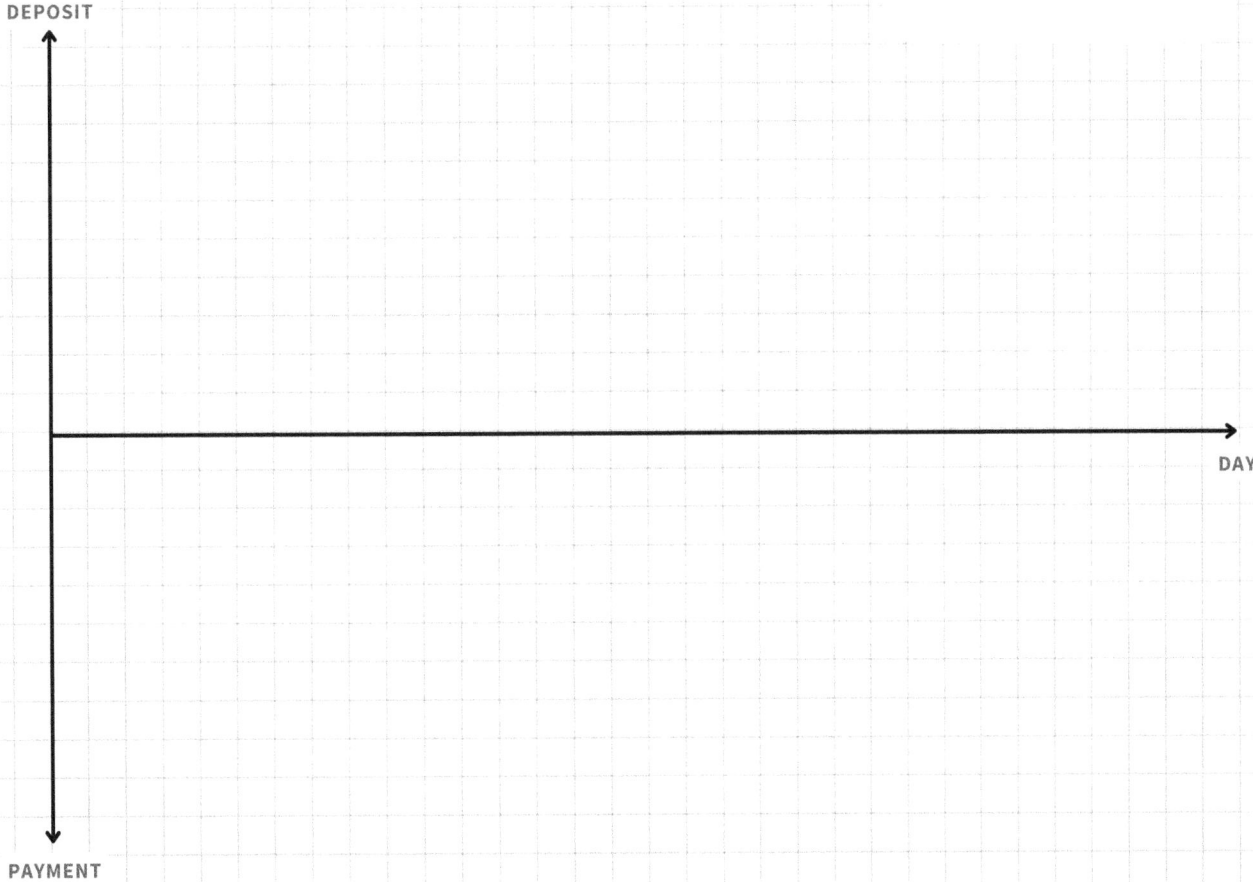

DEPOSIT

DAY

PAYMENT

16

MONTHLY PAYMENTS & DEPOSITS SUMMARY

MONTH : _____

DATE	DAY	PAYMENT / DEBIT (-)	DEPOSIT / CREDIT (+)	TOTAL	NOTES
1					
2					
3					
4					
5					
6					
7					
8					
9					
10					
11					
12					
13					
14					
15					
16					
17					
18					
19					
20					
21					
22					
23					
24					
25					
26					
27					
28					
29					
30					
31					
TOTAL					

MONTHLY PAYMENTS & DEPOSITS CHART

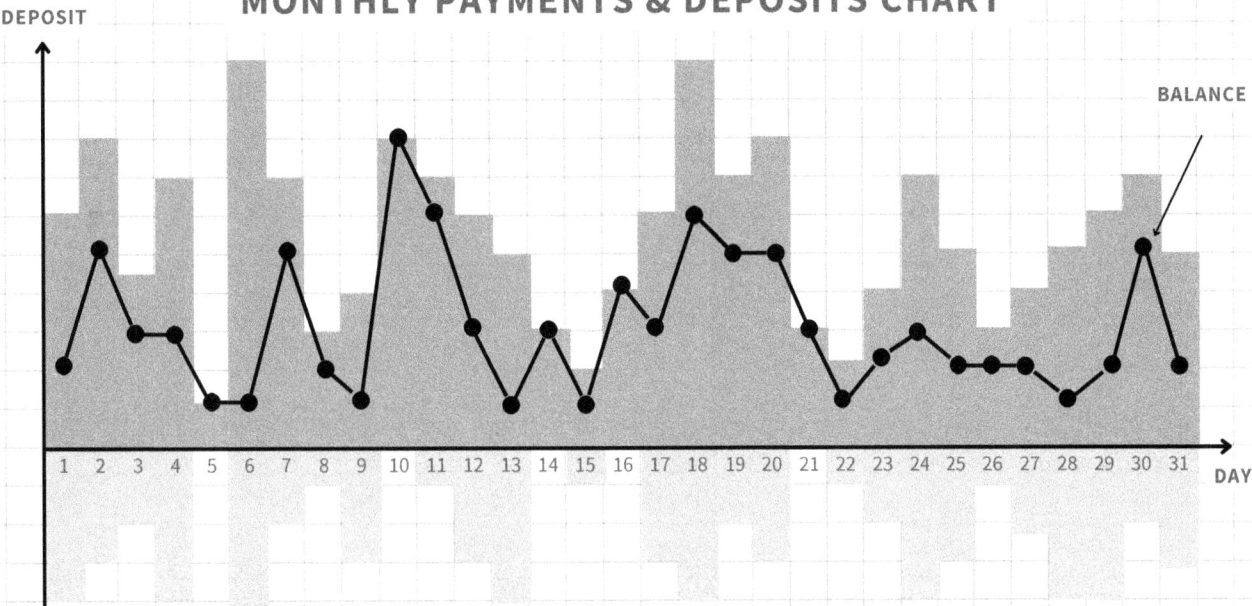

HOW TO:

BUILD YOUR CHART USING YOUR MONTHLY PAYMENTS & DEPOSITS SUMMARY:
- CALCULATE YOUR SCALE USING THE HIGHEST NUMBER IN TERMS OF PAYMENT OR DEPOSIT PER DAY AND DIVIDE IT BY 10 TO GET THE SIZE OF A SQUARE ON THE Y AXIS
- PLOT YOUR TOTAL DAILY DEPOSITS AS POSITIVE BARS ON THE Y-AXIS AND YOUR TOTAL DAILY PAYMENTS AS NEGATIVE BARS ON THE Y-AXIS (DIVIDE DAILY PAYMENT/DEPOSIT BY THE SIZE OF A SQUARE TO FIND THE NUMBER OF SQUARES TO FILL)
- BUILD YOUR BALANCE LINE CHART USING YOUR DAILY TOTAL

MONTH:

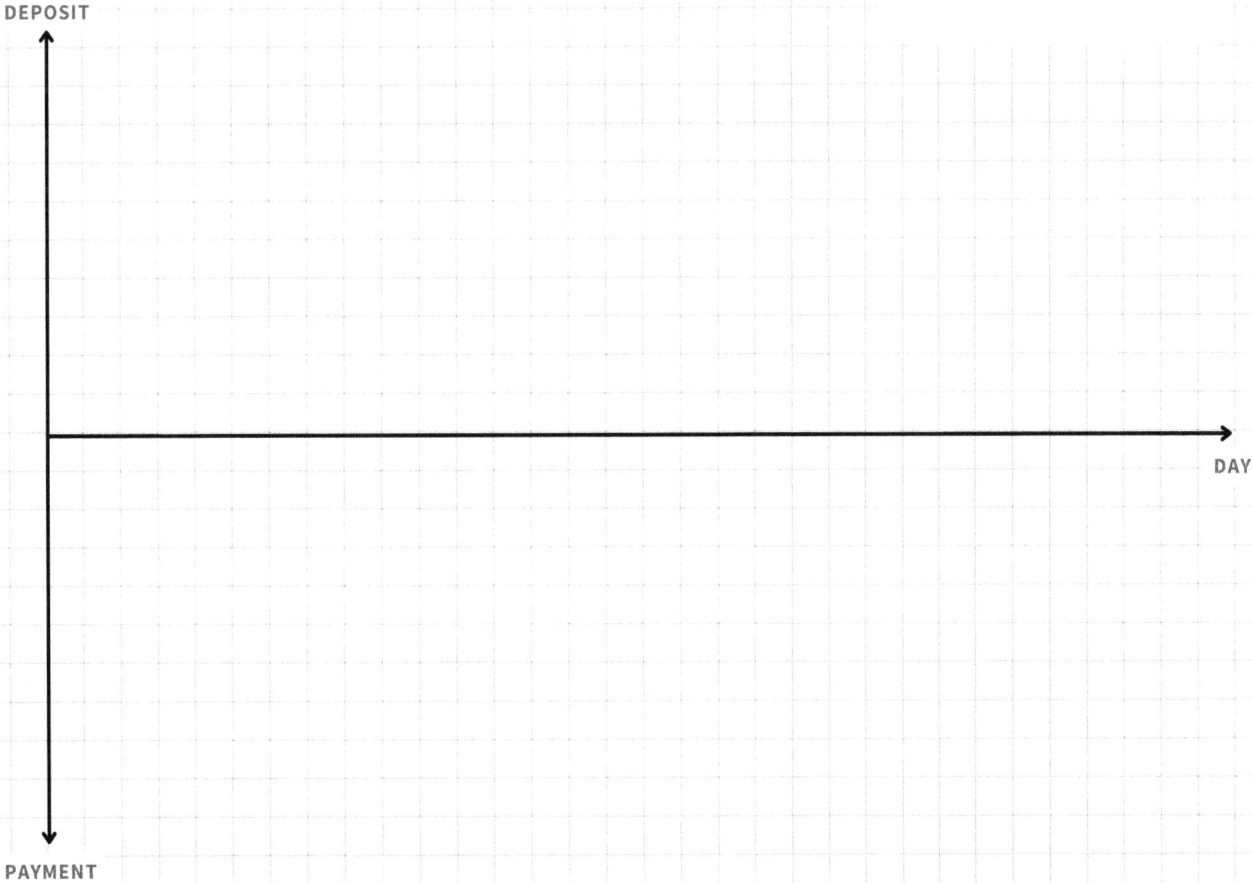

MONTHLY PAYMENTS & DEPOSITS SUMMARY

MONTH : ....

DATE	DAY	PAYMENT / DEBIT (-)	DEPOSIT / CREDIT (+)	TOTAL	NOTES
1					
2					
3					
4					
5					
6					
7					
8					
9					
10					
11					
12					
13					
14					
15					
16					
17					
18					
19					
20					
21					
22					
23					
24					
25					
26					
27					
28					
29					
30					
31					
TOTAL					

MONTHLY PAYMENTS & DEPOSITS CHART

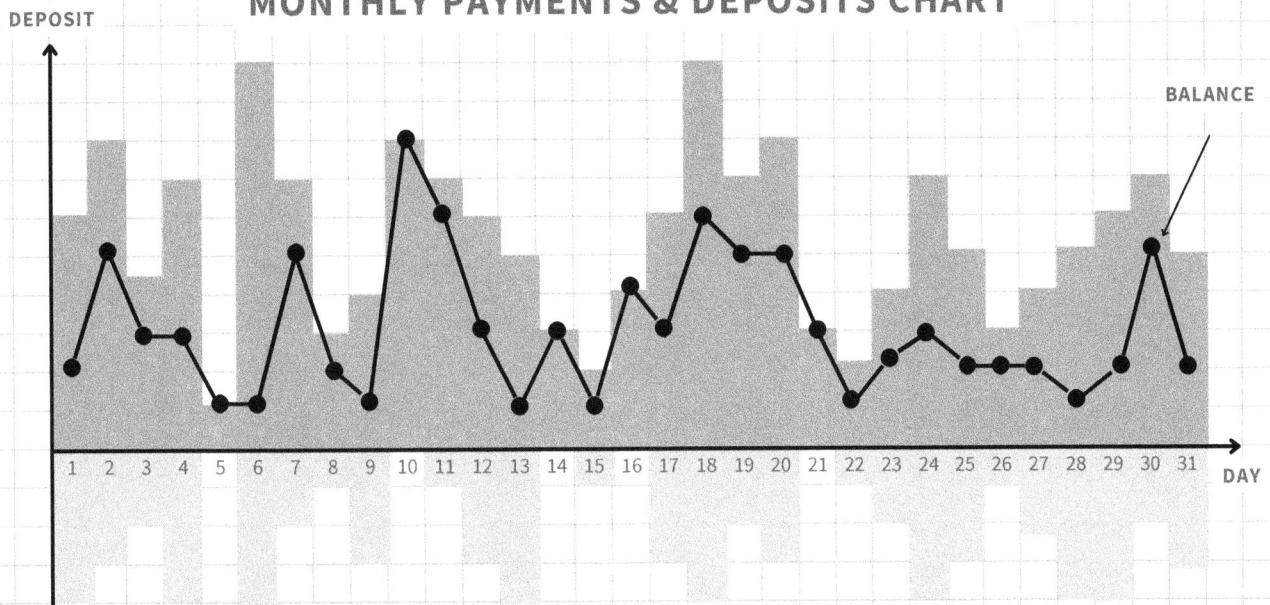

HOW TO:

BUILD YOUR CHART USING YOUR MONTHLY PAYMENTS & DEPOSITS SUMMARY:

- CALCULATE YOUR SCALE USING THE HIGHEST NUMBER IN TERMS OF PAYMENT OR DEPOSIT PER DAY AND DIVIDE IT BY 10 TO GET THE SIZE OF A SQUARE ON THE Y AXIS
- PLOT YOUR TOTAL DAILY DEPOSITS AS POSITIVE BARS ON THE Y-AXIS AND YOUR TOTAL DAILY PAYMENTS AS NEGATIVE BARS ON THE Y-AXIS (DIVIDE DAILY PAYMENT/DEPOSIT BY THE SIZE OF A SQUARE TO FIND THE NUMBER OF SQUARES TO FILL)
- BUILD YOUR BALANCE LINE CHART USING YOUR DAILY TOTAL

MONTH:

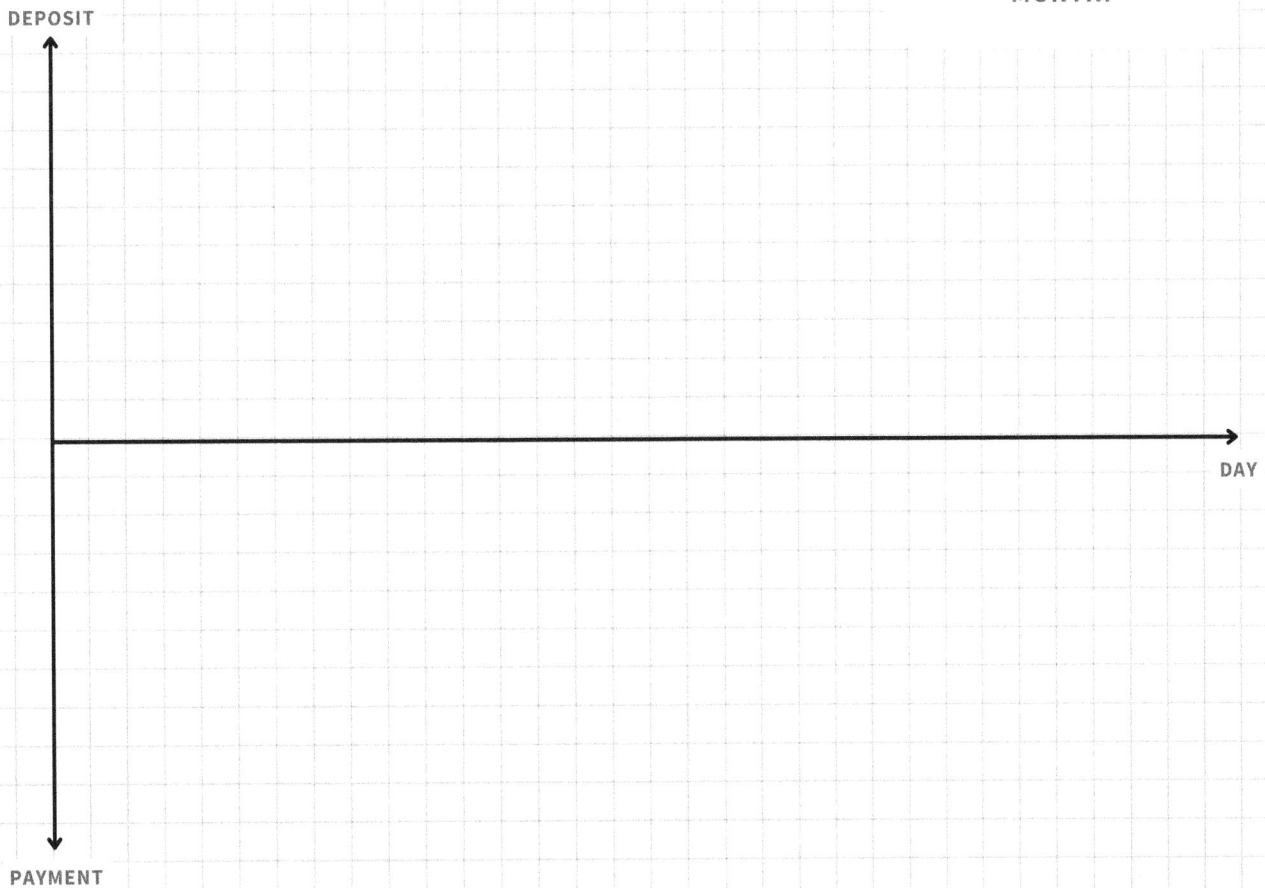

MONTHLY PAYMENTS & DEPOSITS SUMMARY

MONTH : ....

DATE	DAY	PAYMENT / DEBIT (-)	DEPOSIT / CREDIT (+)	TOTAL	NOTES
1					
2					
3					
4					
5					
6					
7					
8					
9					
10					
11					
12					
13					
14					
15					
16					
17					
18					
19					
20					
21					
22					
23					
24					
25					
26					
27					
28					
29					
30					
31					
TOTAL					

MONTHLY PAYMENTS & DEPOSITS CHART

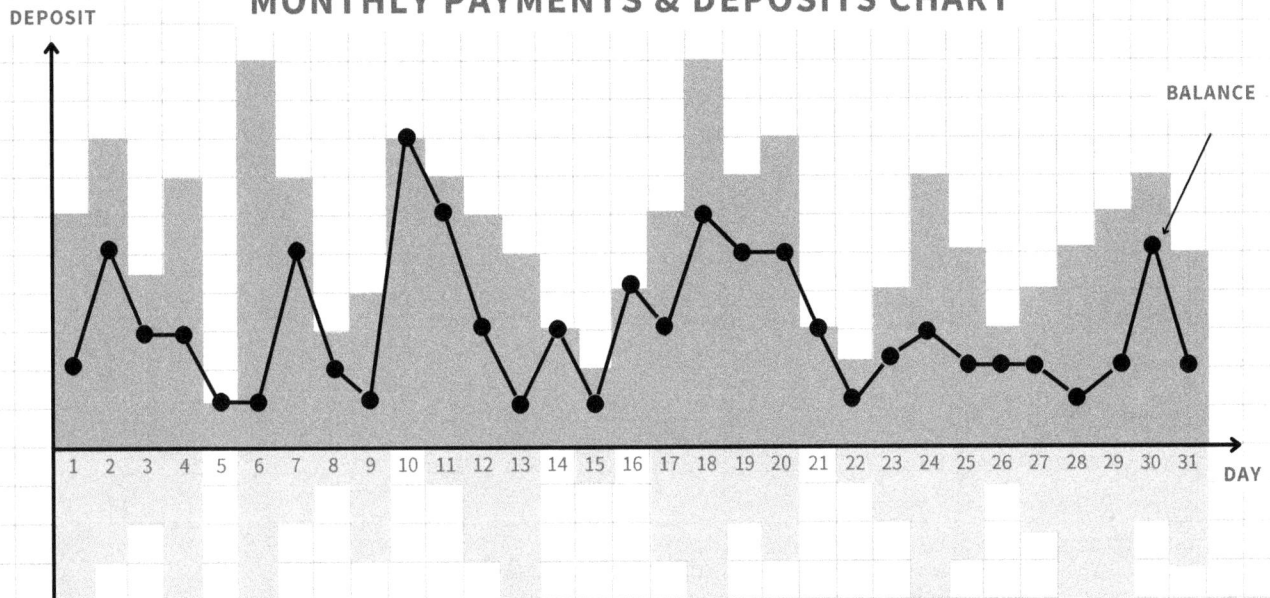

HOW TO:

BUILD YOUR CHART USING YOUR MONTHLY PAYMENTS & DEPOSITS SUMMARY:

- CALCULATE YOUR SCALE USING THE HIGHEST NUMBER IN TERMS OF PAYMENT OR DEPOSIT PER DAY AND DIVIDE IT BY 10 TO GET THE SIZE OF A SQUARE ON THE Y AXIS
- PLOT YOUR TOTAL DAILY DEPOSITS AS POSITIVE BARS ON THE Y-AXIS AND YOUR TOTAL DAILY PAYMENTS AS NEGATIVE BARS ON THE Y-AXIS (DIVIDE DAILY PAYMENT/DEPOSIT BY THE SIZE OF A SQUARE TO FIND THE NUMBER OF SQUARES TO FILL)
- BUILD YOUR BALANCE LINE CHART USING YOUR DAILY TOTAL

MONTH:

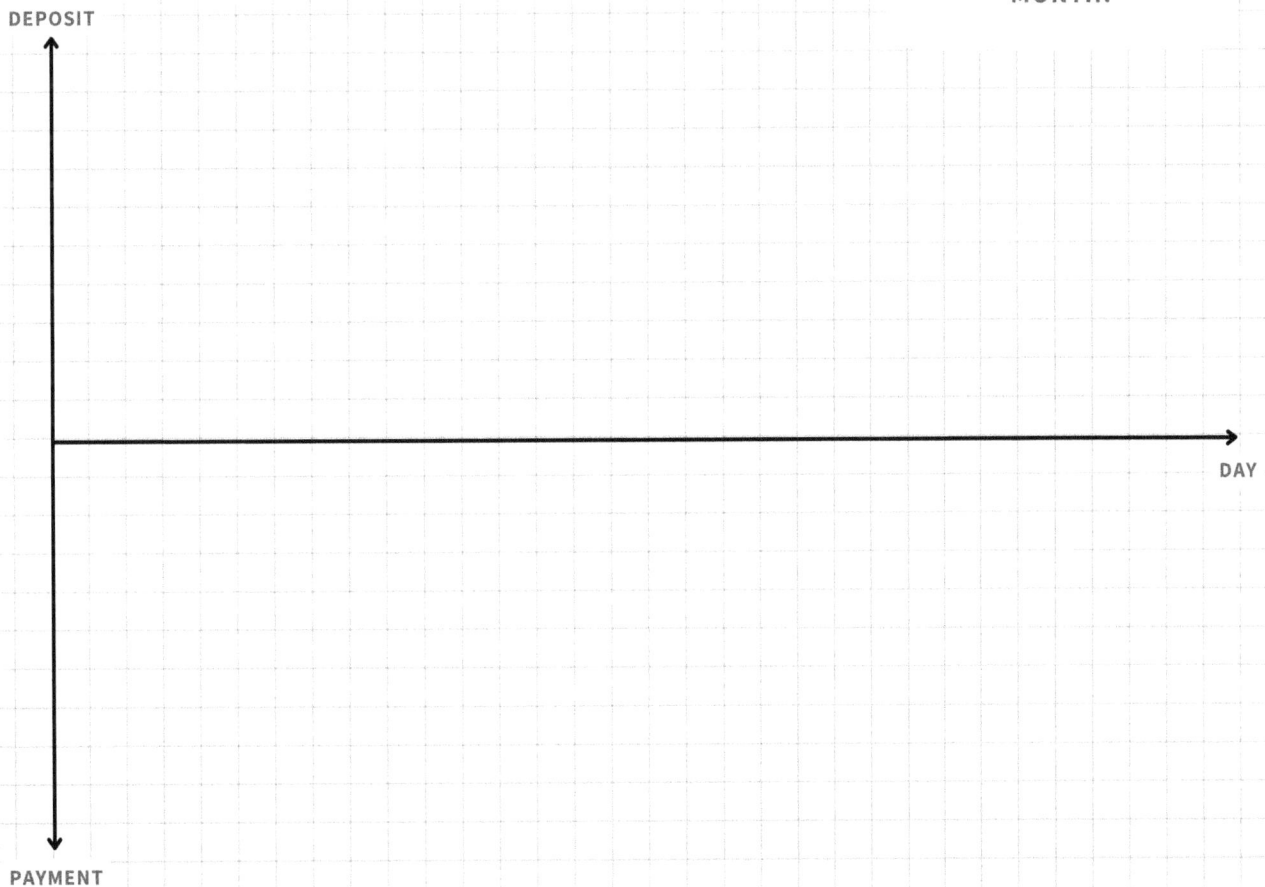

22

MONTHLY PAYMENTS & DEPOSITS SUMMARY

MONTH : ....

DATE	DAY	PAYMENT / DEBIT (-)	DEPOSIT / CREDIT (+)	TOTAL	NOTES
1					
2					
3					
4					
5					
6					
7					
8					
9					
10					
11					
12					
13					
14					
15					
16					
17					
18					
19					
20					
21					
22					
23					
24					
25					
26					
27					
28					
29					
30					
31					
TOTAL					

MONTHLY PAYMENTS & DEPOSITS CHART

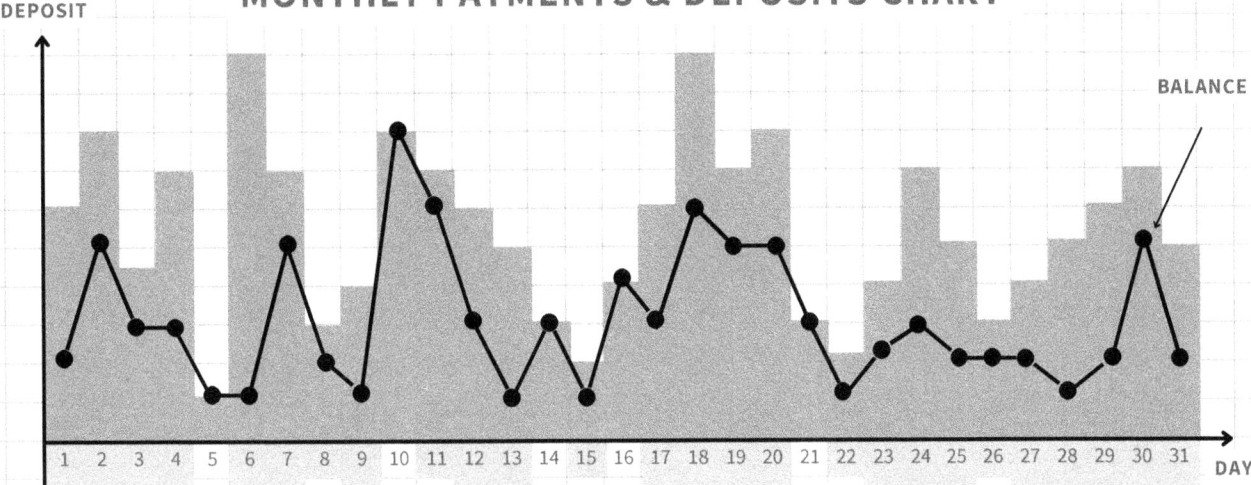

DEPOSIT

BALANCE

1 2 3 4 5 6 7 8 9 10 11 12 13 14 15 16 17 18 19 20 21 22 23 24 25 26 27 28 29 30 31 **DAY**

PAYMENT

HOW TO:
BUILD YOUR CHART USING YOUR MONTHLY PAYMENTS & DEPOSITS SUMMARY:
- CALCULATE YOUR SCALE USING THE HIGHEST NUMBER IN TERMS OF PAYMENT OR DEPOSIT PER DAY AND DIVIDE IT BY 10 TO GET THE SIZE OF A SQUARE ON THE Y AXIS
- PLOT YOUR TOTAL DAILY DEPOSITS AS POSITIVE BARS ON THE Y-AXIS AND YOUR TOTAL DAILY PAYMENTS AS NEGATIVE BARS ON THE Y-AXIS (DIVIDE DAILY PAYMENT/DEPOSIT BY THE SIZE OF A SQUARE TO FIND THE NUMBER OF SQUARES TO FILL)
- BUILD YOUR BALANCE LINE CHART USING YOUR DAILY TOTAL

MONTH:

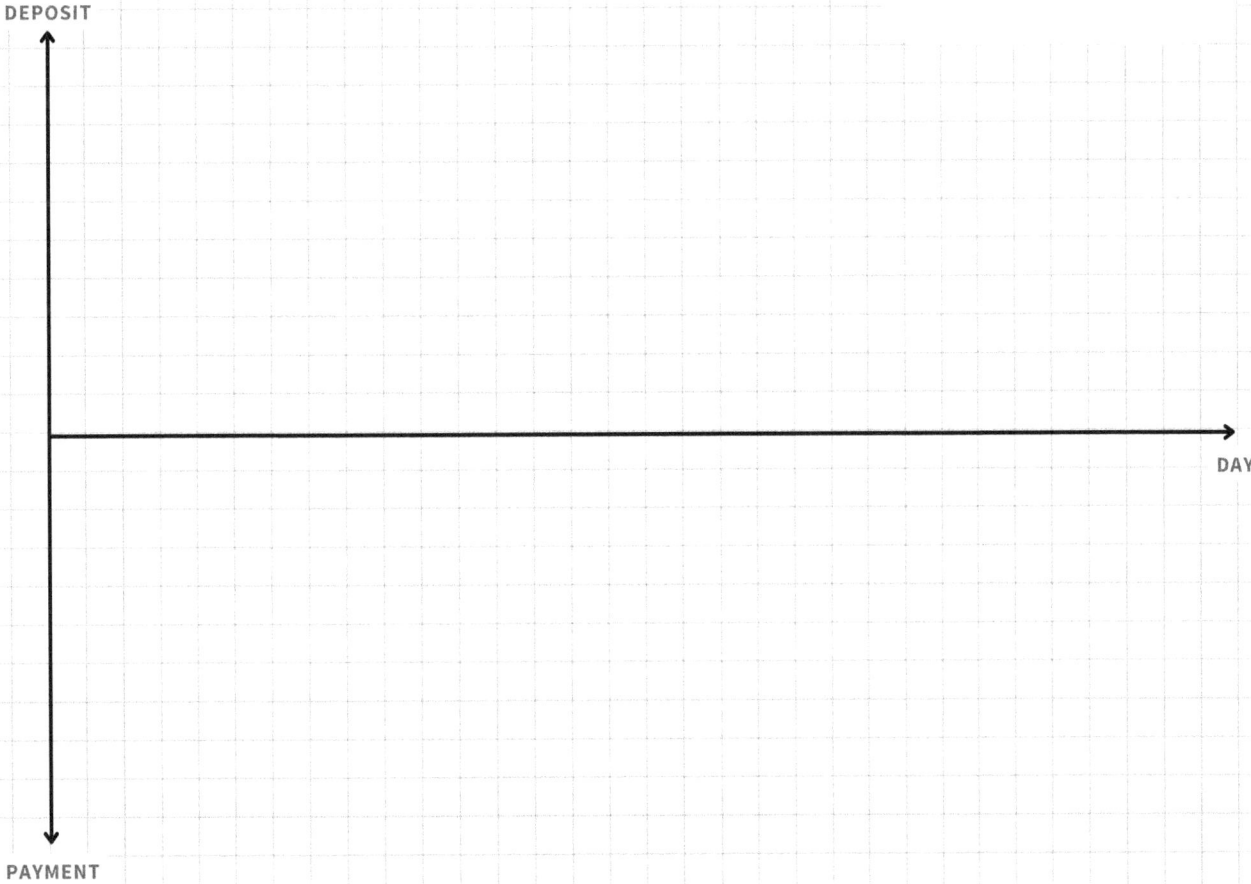

DEPOSIT

DAY

PAYMENT

MONTHLY PAYMENTS & DEPOSITS SUMMARY

MONTH : ....

DATE	DAY	PAYMENT / DEBIT (-)	DEPOSIT / CREDIT (+)	TOTAL	NOTES
1					
2					
3					
4					
5					
6					
7					
8					
9					
10					
11					
12					
13					
14					
15					
16					
17					
18					
19					
20					
21					
22					
23					
24					
25					
26					
27					
28					
29					
30					
31					
TOTAL					

MONTHLY PAYMENTS & DEPOSITS CHART

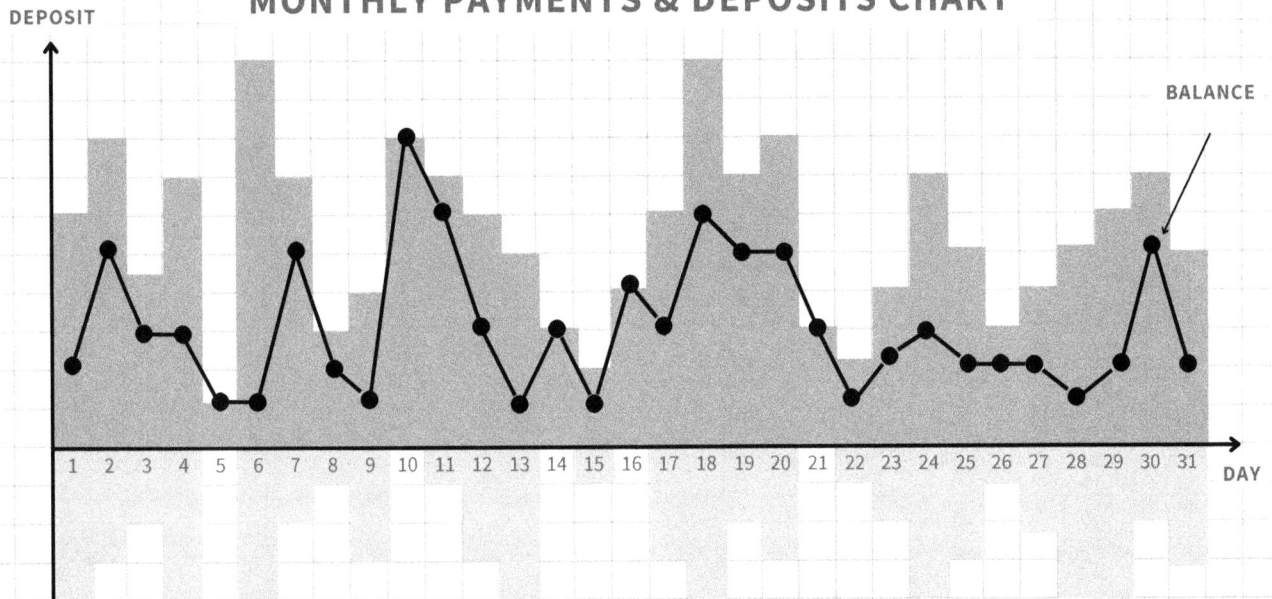

HOW TO:

BUILD YOUR CHART USING YOUR MONTHLY PAYMENTS & DEPOSITS SUMMARY:
- CALCULATE YOUR SCALE USING THE HIGHEST NUMBER IN TERMS OF PAYMENT OR DEPOSIT PER DAY AND DIVIDE IT BY 10 TO GET THE SIZE OF A SQUARE ON THE Y AXIS
- PLOT YOUR TOTAL DAILY DEPOSITS AS POSITIVE BARS ON THE Y-AXIS AND YOUR TOTAL DAILY PAYMENTS AS NEGATIVE BARS ON THE Y-AXIS (DIVIDE DAILY PAYMENT/DEPOSIT BY THE SIZE OF A SQUARE TO FIND THE NUMBER OF SQUARES TO FILL)
- BUILD YOUR BALANCE LINE CHART USING YOUR DAILY TOTAL

MONTH:

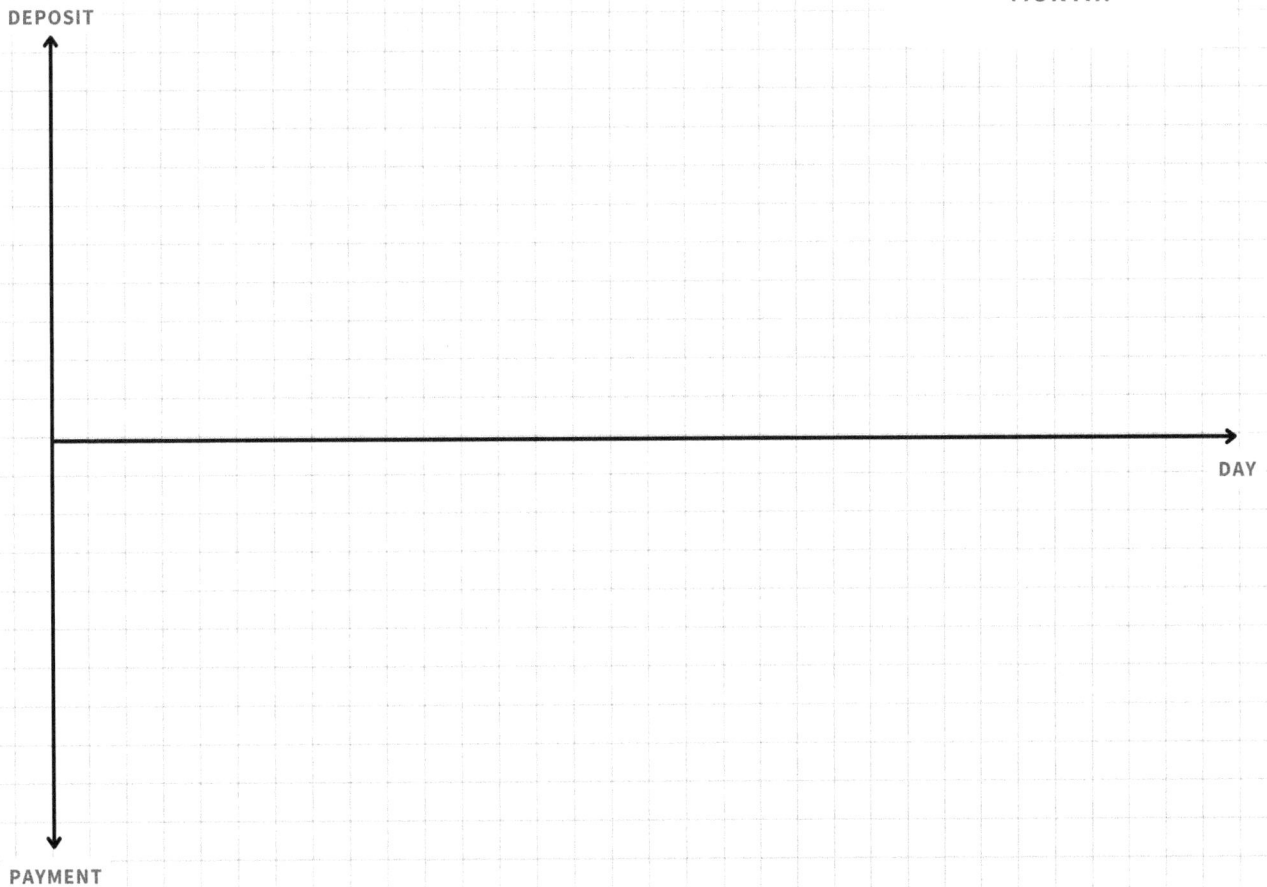

DAILY PAYMENTS & DEPOSITS

MONTH : ....

NO	DATE	DESCRIPTION	ACCOUNT	PAYMENT / DEBIT (-)	DEPOSIT / CREDIT (+)	TOTAL

DAILY PAYMENTS & DEPOSITS

MONTH : ....

NO	DATE	DESCRIPTION	ACCOUNT	PAYMENT / DEBIT (-)	DEPOSIT / CREDIT (+)	TOTAL

DAILY PAYMENTS & DEPOSITS

MONTH : ....

NO	DATE	DESCRIPTION	ACCOUNT	PAYMENT / DEBIT (-)	DEPOSIT / CREDIT (+)	TOTAL

DAILY PAYMENTS & DEPOSITS

MONTH : ....

NO	DATE	DESCRIPTION	ACCOUNT	PAYMENT / DEBIT (-)	DEPOSIT / CREDIT (+)	TOTAL

DAILY PAYMENTS & DEPOSITS

MONTH : ....

NO	DATE	DESCRIPTION	ACCOUNT	PAYMENT / DEBIT (-)	DEPOSIT / CREDIT (+)	TOTAL

DAILY PAYMENTS & DEPOSITS

MONTH : ....

NO	DATE	DESCRIPTION	ACCOUNT	PAYMENT / DEBIT (-)	DEPOSIT / CREDIT (+)	TOTAL

DAILY PAYMENTS & DEPOSITS

MONTH : ....

NO	DATE	DESCRIPTION	ACCOUNT	PAYMENT / DEBIT (-)	DEPOSIT / CREDIT (+)	TOTAL

DAILY PAYMENTS & DEPOSITS

MONTH : ....

NO	DATE	DESCRIPTION	ACCOUNT	PAYMENT / DEBIT (-)	DEPOSIT / CREDIT (+)	TOTAL

DAILY PAYMENTS & DEPOSITS

MONTH : ....

NO	DATE	DESCRIPTION	ACCOUNT	PAYMENT / DEBIT (-)	DEPOSIT / CREDIT (+)	TOTAL

DAILY PAYMENTS & DEPOSITS

MONTH : ....

NO	DATE	DESCRIPTION	ACCOUNT	PAYMENT / DEBIT (-)	DEPOSIT / CREDIT (+)	TOTAL

DAILY PAYMENTS & DEPOSITS

MONTH : ....

NO	DATE	DESCRIPTION	ACCOUNT	PAYMENT / DEBIT (-)	DEPOSIT / CREDIT (+)	TOTAL

DAILY PAYMENTS & DEPOSITS

MONTH : ....

NO	DATE	DESCRIPTION	ACCOUNT	PAYMENT / DEBIT (-)	DEPOSIT / CREDIT (+)	TOTAL

DAILY PAYMENTS & DEPOSITS

MONTH : ....

NO	DATE	DESCRIPTION	ACCOUNT	PAYMENT / DEBIT (-)	DEPOSIT / CREDIT (+)	TOTAL

DAILY PAYMENTS & DEPOSITS

MONTH : ....

NO	DATE	DESCRIPTION	ACCOUNT	PAYMENT / DEBIT (-)	DEPOSIT / CREDIT (+)	TOTAL

DAILY PAYMENTS & DEPOSITS

MONTH : ....

NO	DATE	DESCRIPTION	ACCOUNT	PAYMENT / DEBIT (-)	DEPOSIT / CREDIT (+)	TOTAL

DAILY PAYMENTS & DEPOSITS

MONTH : ....

NO	DATE	DESCRIPTION	ACCOUNT	PAYMENT / DEBIT (-)	DEPOSIT / CREDIT (+)	TOTAL

DAILY PAYMENTS & DEPOSITS

MONTH : ....

NO	DATE	DESCRIPTION	ACCOUNT	PAYMENT / DEBIT (-)	DEPOSIT / CREDIT (+)	TOTAL

DAILY PAYMENTS & DEPOSITS

MONTH : ....

NO	DATE	DESCRIPTION	ACCOUNT	PAYMENT / DEBIT (-)	DEPOSIT / CREDIT (+)	TOTAL

DAILY PAYMENTS & DEPOSITS

MONTH : ....

NO	DATE	DESCRIPTION	ACCOUNT	PAYMENT / DEBIT (-)	DEPOSIT / CREDIT (+)	TOTAL

DAILY PAYMENTS & DEPOSITS

MONTH : ....

NO	DATE	DESCRIPTION	ACCOUNT	PAYMENT / DEBIT (-)	DEPOSIT / CREDIT (+)	TOTAL

DAILY PAYMENTS & DEPOSITS

MONTH : ....

NO	DATE	DESCRIPTION	ACCOUNT	PAYMENT / DEBIT (-)	DEPOSIT / CREDIT (+)	TOTAL

DAILY PAYMENTS & DEPOSITS

MONTH : ....

NO	DATE	DESCRIPTION	ACCOUNT	PAYMENT / DEBIT (-)	DEPOSIT / CREDIT (+)	TOTAL

DAILY PAYMENTS & DEPOSITS

MONTH : ....

NO	DATE	DESCRIPTION	ACCOUNT	PAYMENT / DEBIT (-)	DEPOSIT / CREDIT (+)	TOTAL

DAILY PAYMENTS & DEPOSITS

MONTH : ....

NO	DATE	DESCRIPTION	ACCOUNT	PAYMENT / DEBIT (-)	DEPOSIT / CREDIT (+)	TOTAL

DAILY PAYMENTS & DEPOSITS

MONTH : ....

NO	DATE	DESCRIPTION	ACCOUNT	PAYMENT / DEBIT (-)	DEPOSIT / CREDIT (+)	TOTAL

DAILY PAYMENTS & DEPOSITS

MONTH : ....

NO	DATE	DESCRIPTION	ACCOUNT	PAYMENT / DEBIT (-)	DEPOSIT / CREDIT (+)	TOTAL

DAILY PAYMENTS & DEPOSITS

MONTH : ....

NO	DATE	DESCRIPTION	ACCOUNT	PAYMENT / DEBIT (-)	DEPOSIT / CREDIT (+)	TOTAL

DAILY PAYMENTS & DEPOSITS

MONTH :

NO	DATE	DESCRIPTION	ACCOUNT	PAYMENT / DEBIT (-)	DEPOSIT / CREDIT (+)	TOTAL

DAILY PAYMENTS & DEPOSITS

MONTH : ....

NO	DATE	DESCRIPTION	ACCOUNT	PAYMENT / DEBIT (-)	DEPOSIT / CREDIT (+)	TOTAL

DAILY PAYMENTS & DEPOSITS

MONTH : ....

NO	DATE	DESCRIPTION	ACCOUNT	PAYMENT / DEBIT (-)	DEPOSIT / CREDIT (+)	TOTAL

DAILY PAYMENTS & DEPOSITS

MONTH : ....

NO	DATE	DESCRIPTION	ACCOUNT	PAYMENT / DEBIT (-)	DEPOSIT / CREDIT (+)	TOTAL

DAILY PAYMENTS & DEPOSITS

MONTH : ....

NO	DATE	DESCRIPTION	ACCOUNT	PAYMENT / DEBIT (-)	DEPOSIT / CREDIT (+)	TOTAL

DAILY PAYMENTS & DEPOSITS

MONTH : ....

NO	DATE	DESCRIPTION	ACCOUNT	PAYMENT / DEBIT (-)	DEPOSIT / CREDIT (+)	TOTAL

DAILY PAYMENTS & DEPOSITS

MONTH : ....

NO	DATE	DESCRIPTION	ACCOUNT	PAYMENT / DEBIT (-)	DEPOSIT / CREDIT (+)	TOTAL

DAILY PAYMENTS & DEPOSITS

MONTH : ....

NO	DATE	DESCRIPTION	ACCOUNT	PAYMENT / DEBIT (-)	DEPOSIT / CREDIT (+)	TOTAL

DAILY PAYMENTS & DEPOSITS

MONTH : ....

NO	DATE	DESCRIPTION	ACCOUNT	PAYMENT / DEBIT (-)	DEPOSIT / CREDIT (+)	TOTAL

DAILY PAYMENTS & DEPOSITS

MONTH : ....

NO	DATE	DESCRIPTION	ACCOUNT	PAYMENT / DEBIT (-)	DEPOSIT / CREDIT (+)	TOTAL

DAILY PAYMENTS & DEPOSITS

MONTH : ....

NO	DATE	DESCRIPTION	ACCOUNT	PAYMENT / DEBIT (-)	DEPOSIT / CREDIT (+)	TOTAL

DAILY PAYMENTS & DEPOSITS

MONTH : ....

NO	DATE	DESCRIPTION	ACCOUNT	PAYMENT / DEBIT (-)	DEPOSIT / CREDIT (+)	TOTAL

DAILY PAYMENTS & DEPOSITS

MONTH : ....

NO	DATE	DESCRIPTION	ACCOUNT	PAYMENT / DEBIT (-)	DEPOSIT / CREDIT (+)	TOTAL

DAILY PAYMENTS & DEPOSITS

MONTH : ....

NO	DATE	DESCRIPTION	ACCOUNT	PAYMENT / DEBIT (-)	DEPOSIT / CREDIT (+)	TOTAL

DAILY PAYMENTS & DEPOSITS

MONTH : ....

NO	DATE	DESCRIPTION	ACCOUNT	PAYMENT / DEBIT (-)	DEPOSIT / CREDIT (+)	TOTAL

DAILY PAYMENTS & DEPOSITS

MONTH : ....

NO	DATE	DESCRIPTION	ACCOUNT	PAYMENT / DEBIT (-)	DEPOSIT / CREDIT (+)	TOTAL

DAILY PAYMENTS & DEPOSITS

MONTH : ....

NO	DATE	DESCRIPTION	ACCOUNT	PAYMENT / DEBIT (-)	DEPOSIT / CREDIT (+)	TOTAL

DAILY PAYMENTS & DEPOSITS

MONTH : ....

NO	DATE	DESCRIPTION	ACCOUNT	PAYMENT / DEBIT (-)	DEPOSIT / CREDIT (+)	TOTAL

DAILY PAYMENTS & DEPOSITS

MONTH : ....

NO	DATE	DESCRIPTION	ACCOUNT	PAYMENT / DEBIT (-)	DEPOSIT / CREDIT (+)	TOTAL

DAILY PAYMENTS & DEPOSITS

MONTH : ....

NO	DATE	DESCRIPTION	ACCOUNT	PAYMENT / DEBIT (-)	DEPOSIT / CREDIT (+)	TOTAL

DAILY PAYMENTS & DEPOSITS

MONTH : ....

NO	DATE	DESCRIPTION	ACCOUNT	PAYMENT / DEBIT (-)	DEPOSIT / CREDIT (+)	TOTAL

DAILY PAYMENTS & DEPOSITS

MONTH : ....

NO	DATE	DESCRIPTION	ACCOUNT	PAYMENT / DEBIT (-)	DEPOSIT / CREDIT (+)	TOTAL

DAILY PAYMENTS & DEPOSITS

MONTH : ....

NO	DATE	DESCRIPTION	ACCOUNT	PAYMENT / DEBIT (-)	DEPOSIT / CREDIT (+)	TOTAL

DAILY PAYMENTS & DEPOSITS

MONTH : ....

NO	DATE	DESCRIPTION	ACCOUNT	PAYMENT / DEBIT (-)	DEPOSIT / CREDIT (+)	TOTAL

DAILY PAYMENTS & DEPOSITS

MONTH : ....

NO	DATE	DESCRIPTION	ACCOUNT	PAYMENT / DEBIT (-)	DEPOSIT / CREDIT (+)	TOTAL

DAILY PAYMENTS & DEPOSITS

MONTH : ....

NO	DATE	DESCRIPTION	ACCOUNT	PAYMENT / DEBIT (-)	DEPOSIT / CREDIT (+)	TOTAL

DAILY PAYMENTS & DEPOSITS

MONTH : ....

NO	DATE	DESCRIPTION	ACCOUNT	PAYMENT / DEBIT (-)	DEPOSIT / CREDIT (+)	TOTAL

DAILY PAYMENTS & DEPOSITS

MONTH : ....

NO	DATE	DESCRIPTION	ACCOUNT	PAYMENT / DEBIT (-)	DEPOSIT / CREDIT (+)	TOTAL

DAILY PAYMENTS & DEPOSITS

MONTH : ....

NO	DATE	DESCRIPTION	ACCOUNT	PAYMENT / DEBIT (-)	DEPOSIT / CREDIT (+)	TOTAL

DAILY PAYMENTS & DEPOSITS

MONTH : ....

NO	DATE	DESCRIPTION	ACCOUNT	PAYMENT / DEBIT (-)	DEPOSIT / CREDIT (+)	TOTAL

DAILY PAYMENTS & DEPOSITS

MONTH : ....

NO	DATE	DESCRIPTION	ACCOUNT	PAYMENT / DEBIT (-)	DEPOSIT / CREDIT (+)	TOTAL

DAILY PAYMENTS & DEPOSITS

MONTH : ....

NO	DATE	DESCRIPTION	ACCOUNT	PAYMENT / DEBIT (-)	DEPOSIT / CREDIT (+)	TOTAL

DAILY PAYMENTS & DEPOSITS

MONTH : ....

NO	DATE	DESCRIPTION	ACCOUNT	PAYMENT / DEBIT (-)	DEPOSIT / CREDIT (+)	TOTAL

DAILY PAYMENTS & DEPOSITS

MONTH : ....

NO	DATE	DESCRIPTION	ACCOUNT	PAYMENT / DEBIT (-)	DEPOSIT / CREDIT (+)	TOTAL

DAILY PAYMENTS & DEPOSITS

MONTH : ....

NO	DATE	DESCRIPTION	ACCOUNT	PAYMENT / DEBIT (-)	DEPOSIT / CREDIT (+)	TOTAL

DAILY PAYMENTS & DEPOSITS

MONTH : ....

NO	DATE	DESCRIPTION	ACCOUNT	PAYMENT / DEBIT (-)	DEPOSIT / CREDIT (+)	TOTAL

DAILY PAYMENTS & DEPOSITS

MONTH : ....

NO	DATE	DESCRIPTION	ACCOUNT	PAYMENT / DEBIT (-)	DEPOSIT / CREDIT (+)	TOTAL

DAILY PAYMENTS & DEPOSITS

MONTH : _____

NO	DATE	DESCRIPTION	ACCOUNT	PAYMENT / DEBIT (-)	DEPOSIT / CREDIT (+)	TOTAL

DAILY PAYMENTS & DEPOSITS

MONTH :

NO	DATE	DESCRIPTION	ACCOUNT	PAYMENT / DEBIT (-)	DEPOSIT / CREDIT (+)	TOTAL

DAILY PAYMENTS & DEPOSITS

MONTH : ....

NO	DATE	DESCRIPTION	ACCOUNT	PAYMENT / DEBIT (-)	DEPOSIT / CREDIT (+)	TOTAL

DAILY PAYMENTS & DEPOSITS

MONTH : ....

NO	DATE	DESCRIPTION	ACCOUNT	PAYMENT / DEBIT (-)	DEPOSIT / CREDIT (+)	TOTAL

DAILY PAYMENTS & DEPOSITS

MONTH : ....

NO	DATE	DESCRIPTION	ACCOUNT	PAYMENT / DEBIT (-)	DEPOSIT / CREDIT (+)	TOTAL

DAILY PAYMENTS & DEPOSITS

MONTH : ....

NO	DATE	DESCRIPTION	ACCOUNT	PAYMENT / DEBIT (-)	DEPOSIT / CREDIT (+)	TOTAL

DAILY PAYMENTS & DEPOSITS

MONTH : ....

NO	DATE	DESCRIPTION	ACCOUNT	PAYMENT / DEBIT (-)	DEPOSIT / CREDIT (+)	TOTAL

DAILY PAYMENTS & DEPOSITS

MONTH : ....

NO	DATE	DESCRIPTION	ACCOUNT	PAYMENT / DEBIT (-)	DEPOSIT / CREDIT (+)	TOTAL

DAILY PAYMENTS & DEPOSITS

MONTH : ....

NO	DATE	DESCRIPTION	ACCOUNT	PAYMENT / DEBIT (-)	DEPOSIT / CREDIT (+)	TOTAL

DAILY PAYMENTS & DEPOSITS

MONTH : ....

NO	DATE	DESCRIPTION	ACCOUNT	PAYMENT / DEBIT (-)	DEPOSIT / CREDIT (+)	TOTAL

DAILY PAYMENTS & DEPOSITS

MONTH : ....

NO	DATE	DESCRIPTION	ACCOUNT	PAYMENT / DEBIT (-)	DEPOSIT / CREDIT (+)	TOTAL

DAILY PAYMENTS & DEPOSITS

MONTH : ....

NO	DATE	DESCRIPTION	ACCOUNT	PAYMENT / DEBIT (-)	DEPOSIT / CREDIT (+)	TOTAL

DAILY PAYMENTS & DEPOSITS

MONTH : ....

NO	DATE	DESCRIPTION	ACCOUNT	PAYMENT / DEBIT (-)	DEPOSIT / CREDIT (+)	TOTAL

DAILY PAYMENTS & DEPOSITS

MONTH : ....

NO	DATE	DESCRIPTION	ACCOUNT	PAYMENT / DEBIT (-)	DEPOSIT / CREDIT (+)	TOTAL

DAILY PAYMENTS & DEPOSITS

MONTH : ....

NO	DATE	DESCRIPTION	ACCOUNT	PAYMENT / DEBIT (-)	DEPOSIT / CREDIT (+)	TOTAL

DAILY PAYMENTS & DEPOSITS

MONTH : ....

NO	DATE	DESCRIPTION	ACCOUNT	PAYMENT / DEBIT (-)	DEPOSIT / CREDIT (+)	TOTAL

DAILY PAYMENTS & DEPOSITS

MONTH : _____

NO	DATE	DESCRIPTION	ACCOUNT	PAYMENT / DEBIT (-)	DEPOSIT / CREDIT (+)	TOTAL

DAILY PAYMENTS & DEPOSITS

MONTH : ....

NO	DATE	DESCRIPTION	ACCOUNT	PAYMENT / DEBIT (-)	DEPOSIT / CREDIT (+)	TOTAL

DAILY PAYMENTS & DEPOSITS

MONTH : _____

NO	DATE	DESCRIPTION	ACCOUNT	PAYMENT / DEBIT (-)	DEPOSIT / CREDIT (+)	TOTAL

DAILY PAYMENTS & DEPOSITS

MONTH : ....

NO	DATE	DESCRIPTION	ACCOUNT	PAYMENT / DEBIT (-)	DEPOSIT / CREDIT (+)	TOTAL

DAILY PAYMENTS & DEPOSITS

MONTH : ....

NO	DATE	DESCRIPTION	ACCOUNT	PAYMENT / DEBIT (-)	DEPOSIT / CREDIT (+)	TOTAL

DAILY PAYMENTS & DEPOSITS

MONTH : ....

NO	DATE	DESCRIPTION	ACCOUNT	PAYMENT / DEBIT (-)	DEPOSIT / CREDIT (+)	TOTAL

DAILY PAYMENTS & DEPOSITS

MONTH : ....

NO	DATE	DESCRIPTION	ACCOUNT	PAYMENT / DEBIT (-)	DEPOSIT / CREDIT (+)	TOTAL

DAILY PAYMENTS & DEPOSITS

MONTH : ....

NO	DATE	DESCRIPTION	ACCOUNT	PAYMENT / DEBIT (-)	DEPOSIT / CREDIT (+)	TOTAL

DAILY PAYMENTS & DEPOSITS

MONTH : ....

NO	DATE	DESCRIPTION	ACCOUNT	PAYMENT / DEBIT (-)	DEPOSIT / CREDIT (+)	TOTAL

DAILY PAYMENTS & DEPOSITS

MONTH : ....

NO	DATE	DESCRIPTION	ACCOUNT	PAYMENT / DEBIT (-)	DEPOSIT / CREDIT (+)	TOTAL

www.ingramcontent.com/pod-product-compliance
Lightning Source LLC
Chambersburg PA
CBHW051758200326
41597CB00025B/4599